Lord, If I Ever Needed You It's Now!

Lord, If I Ever Needed You It's Now!

Creath Davis

Palm Desert, CA 92261-3229

Grand Rapids, Michigan 49516

Copyright © 1981 by Creath Davis

All rights reserved. No portion of this book may be used or reproduced in any form without written permission of the publisher except in the case of brief quotations within critical articles and reviews.

Person to Person Books
ISBN: 0-88021-030-3

Baker Book House
ISBN: 0-8010-2968-6

Second printing, August 1987

Library of Congress Catalog Card Number 81-83584

Printed in the United States of America

To the men who have met at Palo Petroleum, Inc. for Bible Study and Sharing on Monday mornings for the past three years and who have prayed for me throughout the writing of this book: Jim Graham, Lonnie Holotik, Rob Moore, Larry Honea, James Ostler, Larry Phillips, Victor Moossy, Brooks Gremmels, Dale Johnson, Bill Loring-Clark, Steve Cromeens, Rusty Brittain, Bill Walker, Dave Hogan, Pat Bolin, John Dillon, David Kalish, Max Schnallinger, Mart Higginbotham, Griff Hendon, Jim Holotik, Mike Denton, Jim Rutledge and Tom McWhorter.

TABLE OF CONTENTS

Part I	An Incredible Story	19
	1. An Agony Too Deep for Words	21
Part II	The Person	37
	2. What Am I Bringing to the Struggle?	39
Part III	The Process	51
	3. Let the Heart Speak	53
	4. There Must Be Some Mistake	59
	5. Why Me?	63
	6. Promises	73
	7. What's the Use?	79
	8. Acceptance	87
Part IV	THE HOPE	95
	9. What Can I Expect from God?	97
Part V	Personal Reflection/Group Interaction	115

Grateful acknowledgment is made to the following for permission to use copyright material:

The Seabury Press
> From A GRIEF OBSERVED by C. S. Lewis. Copyright © 1961 by N. W. Clerk. Used by permission of The Seabury Press, Inc.

Chosen Books
> From BEYOND OURSELVES by Catherine Marshall. Copyright © 1961. Published by Chosen Books, Lincoln, VA 22078. Used by permission.

Zondervan Publishing House
> From JONI by Joni Eareckson and Joe Musser. Copyright © 1976 by Joni Eareckson and Joe Musser. Used by permission.

Zondervan Publishing House
> From HOW TO WIN OVER DEPRESSION by Tim LaHaye. Copyright © 1974 by the Zondervan Corporation. Used by permission.

Fleming H. Revell Company
> From AFFLICTION by Edith Schaeffer. Copyright © 1979. Published by Fleming H. Revell Company. Used by permission.

Faber and Faber Ltd.
> From A GRIEF OBSERVED by C. S. Lewis. Copyright © 1966. Published by Faber and Faber Ltd. Used by permission.

Word Books, Publisher
> From TRACKS OF A FELLOW STRUGGLER by John Claypool. Copyright © 1979. Used by permission of Word Books, Publisher, Waco, Texas 76703

Harper & Row, Publishers, Inc.
> From ACHIEVING REAL HAPPINESS by Kenneth Hildebrand. Copyright © 1955 credited to Sydney J. Harris. Used by permission.

Zondervan Publishing House
> From WHERE IS GOD WHEN IT HURTS by Philip Yancey. Copyright © 1977 by the Zondervan Corporation. Used by permission.

ACKNOWLEDGMENTS

The Christian Concern Foundation fellowship which has been in existence for sixteen years has provided so many rich relationships and experiences for discovering the transforming grace of God readily available in any and all circumstances that this book must be seen as their witness.

Without the efforts of my wife, Verdell, who labored with me in the writing of this book; Robert Williams who gave some much needed objective editing; and Debbie Vaughan, my secretary, who typed and retyped this manuscript, this witness would never have taken written form.

A special thanks to our staff at Kaleo Lodge: Preston and Johnnie Ree Robichaux, Bobbie Neely and Andrea Hooter who are Christ's servants to scores of people week after week.

A WORD OF THANKS

To George Clark and Jodie Thompson who met with me at noon on Thursdays for almost three years for sharing and Bible Study.

To the Bible study group which met at Jodie and Dottie Thompson's home—Hugo and Gail Schoellkopf, Maury and

Diane Purnell, Jim and Carol Mason, Allan and Mara Schoellkopf.

To the Bible study groups which met at the homes of George and Miley Busiek, Russell and Lisa Johnson, Jack and Nance Wilson, Dick and Ellen Sayles, Clint and Anne Murchison, Lynn and Peggy Newman, Don and Janie McKay, Ron and Betty Wideman, Jack and Fran Davis, Ron and Barbara Grusendorf, Jim and Pam Graham, Lonnie and Lorry Holotik, Taylor and Vickie Fuller, John J. Stasney, III, Vickie Hill, Rusty and Mary Beth Coffee.

To those individuals who have ministered to me in a significant way during the writing of this book: Roy and Janis Coffee, Dr. John Newport, Ray Lawson, Jim and Nedra Williams, Bob and Janie Spencer, Charles and Kathleen Denman, Bill Hunter, Leonard Holloway, Dick and Ellen Rowe Philips, Homer Walkup, David McKinnon, Glen Hinckley, Gwynne Pollock, Dr. Hudson T. Armerding, Chaplain Pat Patterson, David and Janet Reed, Steve and Becky Lowe, Tom and Carole McBride, Chris Sharp, Michael and Paula Quinn, Ray and Sharon Powell, Dee Northington, Dottie Pierce, Steve and Eta Lankford, James Barnett, Ione Lewis, Joel Williams, Paul Lee, Connie Norton, Ann Clark, Wayne Snyder, Mike and Nancy Smith, Charley Harris, George Soltau, Austin Anderson, John and Denise Farmer, Willard Thompson, Allan and Sharon Bryant, Dave Powell, Dub and Earlene Chambers, Dr. James Pleitz, Dr. Clayton Bell, Chuck and Lois Scheckner, Paul and Patsy Bellington, Darryl Gumm, Jim and Terry Wilson, Randy Ashcraft, Judi Wilson, James and Jean Hamilton, David and Frankie Hartman, John and Jo McCoy, Bill and Candy Hill, Dick and Sylvia Gilmore, Laden Stroud, Jerry and Wally Fulwiler, Len Sunukjian, D.L. and Emma Riley, Elmer Fisher, Doyle and Cookie

Clawson, the late Mickey Warlick and Shirley, Bill and Patsy Bragg, Pete and Frances Chantillis and Walter and Lou Ann Elwell.

To my oil patch friends—Cecil (Tiny) Wilson, Bob Prentice, Noel King, Pat Patterson, J. D. Goble, Roland Jones, Pete Cantrell, Bill Updegraff.

Finally, a word of thanks to my publisher Ron Haynes and Carolyn for their enthusiastic response to this manuscript.

FOREWORD

Each of us will face at some point in our journey a struggle or struggles which will appear to be absolutely insurmountable. In such a place we may feel that all we have known which has made life good and worthwhile is being taken from us. Questions come to our mind rather quickly in times like these: What can we do? How can we cope? Is there anyone who understands our plight? Is there anyone who cares?

I am glad there are concrete and positive answers available to any of us who are willing to take the biblical insight seriously. The Bible makes clear the fact that we do live in a fallen world where pain and suffering abound, but it is not a world abandoned by God nor void of His grace and power.

We *can* do something! We can deal honestly with the reality of our trauma and can discover why and how we can trust the God who came to us in Jesus Christ to do the miraculous in our life.

Creath Davis
Dallas, Texas
June 1981

INTRODUCTION

This book is a *book of hope*. It has been written to answer the question, "What can we expect from God when the going gets tough?" It does not deal primarily with the issue of death but rather with facing *any devastating crisis or struggle*. Both biblical and contemporary models have been used to give a realistic perspective for responding honestly and openly to God, who is always reliable but not always understood.

The seeds for this book were planted, in part, by the scores of people who have shared their anguish with me as a minister and counselor and, in part, by my own struggle to understand the difference the gospel claims to make in the practical arena of one's everyday life. However, the big push to get on with this project came when a good friend shared with my wife and me the remarkable story related in the first chapter. I saw in Virginia's experience many different facets of God's grace, reflected so magnificently that I knew this must be shared.

There are five sections in this book. The first is the story of one person's discovery of the "sufficiency of God's grace" experienced in different ways at different times. The second section deals with the *person* entering the struggle and the significance of what we do and what we become as we open or close ourselves to life. The third section deals with the personal and emotional trauma inherent in every major crisis. It is intended to help the person express and work through his deep feelings without fear but with a progressive movement toward genuine wholeness. The fourth section deals with the *hope* which belongs to every pilgrim of faith. It is the kind of hope which rests solidly on God being God whether He moves to rescue us, calls us to collaborate with Him, or simply enables us to endure and in the enduring to know what true greatness is. The final section provides questions for personal reflection and small group dialogue. It is divided into nine sessions to coincide with the chapters in the book.

In essence this book is a witness to the truth of Paul's statement in Romans, "We know that in all things God works for the good of those who love him."

PART I

An Incredible Story

CHAPTER ONE

An Agony Too Deep for Words

> You never know how much you really believe anything until its truth or falsehood becomes a matter of life and death to you.[1]
>
> C. S. Lewis

I never met Virginia, yet her life and death affected me in such a way that I feel the need to share it. Her story is the story of how one finite human being dealt with the severest of struggles and discovered that faith in the infinite personal God, revealed in Jesus Christ, is incredibly adequate in all situations.

I first heard of Virginia when my wife related to me a conversation she had with her friend Joanie. Virginia was one of Joanie's closest friends who, four years earlier had experienced a miraculous healing from cancer but finally lost a later similar bout with the dreaded disease. Along with her grief, Joanie expressed her amazement at what had happened to all the people Virginia had touched in her death. One of life's most perplexing yet profound realities had been clearly demonstrated to Joanie—*that good can come from the ugliest and most devastating kind of cir-*

cumstances. Not that the circumstance itself was good, but the changes which occurred in the people who walked through the darkness gave unmistakable evidence of the presence of God who enabled them to endure an agony too deep for words!

Having been touched personally by this family's suffering, I asked permission to tell part of their story here. What I share will be incomplete for at least two reasons: first, no one can fully comprehend or share adequately another's agony or joy; secondly, the drama is still in progress at the time of this writing and any attempts to write the word "finished" over this story would be premature.

What happened to Virginia belongs to every pilgrim of faith and even to the skeptics who cannot in their unbelief avoid the maladies common to mankind any more than can we who believe. Suffering is an undeniable part of the human scene which will not be permanently avoided by any of us. Yet the difference between *belief* and *unbelief* in dealing with suffering is great. The pain and the anxiety may not be lessened, but what becomes of us as we struggle with the cup life gives us to drink will reveal the mystery of a benevolent God who not only uses our suffering to enlarge our capacity for life, but who also *participates* in our suffering. In describing the radical change that Christ had brought in his own life, Paul says that, "the things which were so important before seem worthless compared to what I have found in Christ."[2] He goes on to say that what he prizes now is the opportunity "to experience Christ in the power of his resurrection and in the fellowship of his suffering. . . ."[3]

While most of us are delighted with the prospect of *experiencing Christ in the power of his resurrection,* we do not even like to think about sharing in the fellowship of His suffering. The ecstasy we crave; the agony we fear. But suffering can create a fellowship, or better translated, *an intimacy* that no other experience in life affords, especially an intimacy with God. As long as I hold on to my suffering as *my suffering* I will only experience loneliness and despair. But once I open my suffering to God so that it becomes His suffering too, then I am no longer alone and our suffering together becomes redemptive. When we realize that nowhere in all the world is the agony and pain that we feel felt as deeply nor as keenly as it is in the heart of God, and that the promise of the Living Christ is to never forsake us, then we will truly know that our suffering is His, too.

It is this realization which enables us to believe that there is purpose in our suffering even if we cannot identify or articulate clearly what that purpose is. It helps enormously to know that our suffering is *not* simply blind happenstance in a cold, impersonal universe.

Virginia's story is one of warmth and courage which demonstrates most clearly the meaning faith can bring from the toughest circumstances life can present. She would be upset with us if we failed to let her be human in sharing her pilgrimage. In fact, it is because her humanity was revealed and, in a significant way, transformed that her death radiates hope rather than despair.

It was not perfection but *peace* that Virginia found at the end of her journey—the kind of peace that bears an unmistakable witness to the presence of God in a human life! It was Christ who said, "Peace I leave with you; my peace I give you . . ."[4] It is when we stand in the presence of the Lord God Almighty and know that we are loved, forgiven, and made to be His child that there is nothing left to fear—not the past, nor the present, nor the future.

Let me describe Virginia so you can better understand and appreciate her gift to us. Virginia was a woman in love with life, with Ted her husband, and with young Ted and Francy, her children. Life held much promise for her. Not that everything had always been easy up until her illness, but from the perspective of the incredibly hard place she finally had to walk everything else seemed easy. She and Ted had many of the "normal" conflicts that come in most journeys toward intimacy in marriage. However, as the years passed, their lives became so intertwined that they truly were "one flesh."

There were the joys and struggles which go along with being the mother of two. She thrived on the challenges that came with being a parent and always held great aspirations for her children. One recurring battle she fought in this area was her tendency to be over-protective. Francy spoke of her as a "doting" mother. Most parents will readily identify with her because it is not easy to release our children for their own risky journey into adulthood. But release them we must!

Virginia was a very aware, creative, feminine person. She loved pretty clothes, antiques and working in women's organizations. She had a mind of her own and a temper that could flare when she was pushed, yet she was basically a peacemaker who disliked dwelling on the negative aspects of life. Virginia could see beauty in the world around her and could create artistic displays with the simple things she collected on walks at the beach and at their farm—"a frustrated artist," her daughter called her.

How strange it is that when life is without any major struggle we tend to operate under the illusion that this is the way life will be for us indefinitely. From such illusion we are tempted to take for granted the very things which make life rich—our families and friends, our health and our opportunities to enjoy life and to express our own uniqueness in God's world. If life remained on a completely even keel perhaps we would never discover the depth of our own being or of God's, nor would we appreciate the incomprehensible mysteries that are all about us. Even with this knowledge most of us, if not all, would still choose the calm over the storm. None of us would knowingly invite pain, agony or struggle into our lives. Yet all the greats in history owe a significant part of their greatness to the battles they fought which forced them to become more than they ever would have been without the struggle. Still we would probably prefer a little less greatness in order to enjoy a little more tranquility. But reality does not always offer us a choice between trauma and tranquility. The only real choice seems to be *what we do with what comes.* Even a casual observer of life is aware that tragedy can strike swiftly and without warning. One day life may be sweet and the next day bitter. What we choose to do with the *bitter* reveals more about us than any other dimension of our lives.

The drama of agony started while the family was on vacation at Lake Texoma. Virginia felt a lump in her stomach which gave her enough concern to have it checked out when she came back to Dallas. It turned out to be an enlarged ovary. The first test revealed malignancy and exploratory surgery was performed. The doctor told Ted that he had removed all he could without leaving her paralyzed. That night Ted, in tears and on his knees, asked God, "Why? Why is this happening to Virginia?"

The shock of such things is too much for us. We cannot understand it, much less accept it at first. Since God gives us permission to wrestle with our questions and our emotions we need desperately to give to one another that same permission. Too often those of us who are on the periphery of the hurt are threatened by our friend's agony and try different ways to bolster him. We may not want him to question God or express anger. Sometimes we may even try to calm another's spirit by saying that it is God's will, which not only fails to solve the problem but may cause that person to feel alienated from his source of greatest hope. The adversities of life are mysterious. In all probability the more we try to explain them or fix blame and responsibility, the further we move from the truth.

God did not withdraw from Ted just because he questioned Him. In fact there is more honest faith in an act of questioning than in silent submission. *Implicit in the very act of asking is the faith that some light can be given.* Of course, Ted did not only ask *why,* he also asked God to heal his wife. God answered his and Virginia's prayers, for Virginia later shared with Ted that she had asked the Lord for some additional years to finish rearing their children, Ted, then age 17 and 15-year-old Francy. He gave her those years! The Scriptures encourage us again and again to make our request known to the Lord. He never turns a deafened ear to us and He always answers our prayer in the light of His eternal purpose.

The next series of tests brought both surprise and relief to the family. The tests turned out to be negative, which had the emotional impact of lifting the weight of the world from their shoulders. *It was a miracle* that even the doctors could not explain. The area that had first appeared cancerous now was benign. What thanksgiving the whole family experienced. They were certain that God had wrought a miracle, and no one would dispute it! Even so, as a precaution Virginia was given cobalt treatments. She also submitted herself to strenuous examinations periodically by physicians who were making a special study of her case. She felt that if they could learn something from her

An Agony Too Deep for Words

situation that would help someone else, then the unpleasant ordeal would be worthwhile.

That Christmas the whole family went skiing. Life was returning to normal. Virginia and Ted, Francy and young Ted had four good years before the illness returned. But unfortunately, it did return. God can and does heal us, but the awesome truth is that at some point God's healing mercies for our bodies cease and His grace for dying begins. The Scriptures declare, "... a man is destined to die once, and after that to face judgement."[5] The only exception will be those who are alive when Christ returns and since no man knows for certain when that time will be, there is little reason for us to count on that for our escape. Our perfection in body, mind and soul awaits the world to come.

Virginia began to feel ill and went for another examination. The doctor told her he was afraid her old problem was back. This infuriated Virginia so much that she called him "Mr. Gloom" and said, "Why don't you think positive until you are sure?"

I wonder what would be your reaction or mine if a doctor brought us a report which confirmed that we had some dreaded disease. Those would be horrible words that would shake our very roots.

Facing the reality of your own death is one of life's toughest assignments. Virginia wanted desperately to live and she fought hard and long to make it. After all, she was young, she loved Ted and did not want to leave him, and she did not want to die before Francy was married or before young Ted was established in his own life pursuits. She was losing so much and felt that she was leaving so much unfinished.

In the midst of the struggle Virginia found some resources in her relationship with Jesus Christ that made a remarkable difference in the way she walked through the darkness. Her faith did not eliminate the pain or the cancer or keep her from losing her hair when she took the chemotherapy treatment. But it did enable her to find a peace which transcended the storm and allowed hope to flourish.

It was not her nature to complain so she always sounded better than she was when anyone talked with her, including her doctors. When Ted confronted her with what she was doing, her remark was, "Who wants to talk to a sick person?" She cheered up those who came to encourage her. This was her way of keeping her chin up in the face of great distress. We actually receive what we attempt to give, and by encouraging those who came to sympathize with her she was encouraged herself.

As in every serious illness, there were a multitude of crises which Virginia had to face. She struggled with each one as every fighter would. When the doctor told her that she would have to have a colostomy her response was, "I would rather die than have a colostomy." Ted told her that she did not have that right and she agreed. After she had the surgery her remark to Ted was, "This isn't as hideous as I thought it would be. I was afraid of the way you and the children would take it." The dignity of every person is every bit as important as their physical well being, and to many it is more important. Virginia at first saw the colostomy as a serious threat to her worth in the eyes of her family. It was a tremendous relief to discover that it in no way diminished her value as a person.

There were many talks which took place during those last five months. It was on one of those occasions that she shared with Ted her prayer four years earlier that the Lord give her the time to finish rearing her children. She felt that He had given her the four years extension in response to that request. Now her youngest was in college. In that dialogue with Ted, Virginia celebrated those four years as a gracious gift from the Lord rather than begrudging the loss of the years ahead with the family.

The brief periods that she was able to be at home were rich times for her. She would sometimes laugh about how she walked like a crippled bug. Much of the time she was really on top of the situation and, out of great strength, ministered to those around her. However, there were periods when the bleakness of her situation would make her angry. One such occasion was when she could not keep her food down for more than 30 minutes. She cried and said, "I'm so tired of all this. How long is this going to go on?"

Her suffering seemed endless yet she battled it to the finish, because one thing she was not—a quitter. And in her fight with death she touched life in a way that freed the best within and made the end, which was imminent, hold the promise of an incredibly new beginning.

Letting go of what she could not hold on to was part of the process which in the end allowed her such peace. Ted shared with me through his tears the conversation he and Virginia had the night she released the family. She knew the end was near and did what she felt she must. She said, "It doesn't look as if I am going to get any better. So today I released you all to God. I've had a hard time coming to this, but now I know that you three will be okay if I don't make it." Virginia continued, "It's a strange feeling to let go of everything you love and hold dear." With this Ted embraced her as they both wept in each others' arms.

On another occasion she told Ted, Francy and Ted, Jr. that they would have to let her go; as hard as that may be, they just had to do it.

When her friend Joanie would visit during those last

weeks Virginia would talk freely about death. On one of those visits she said, "I am not going to survive this illness, but I don't dwell on it because I don't know when. But I do wonder what it will be like to die. In a way I am excited, except for having to leave Ted and the kids."

This was more than Joanie could handle and she began to cry and say, "Why? Why does it have to be you?"

Virginia's reply was one that came from a woman who had found God to be so real in the midst of her agony that she had lost her fear. "Why *not* me?" was her response. Those three words were not weak resignation but profound acceptance.

Joanie said to me, "I envied her at that point. She had peace of mind that is better than any physical blessings. She was at peace with God and death to her was not a dreaded end, but a new beginning."

Three weeks later, after finishing a needlepoint project that she had her heart set on completing, Virginia died.

In her death she gave us the gift of hope, not despair; of joy, not remorse; and of unbelievable courage. For in that enormous struggle she came to know most intimately the One who said, ". . . He who believes in me will live, even though he dies; and whoever lives and believes in me will never die. Do you believe this?"[6] . . . Virginia did. Peace, as Virginia experienced it, does not always come to everyone who struggles with dying. *Death is man's last enemy.* Paul, the Apostle, made that fact clear when he wrote, "The last enemy to be destroyed is death."[7] Therefore we need not treat death in any other vein than that of being an ugly enemy. For this reason dying usually does not come easy. We were created for life, and our bodies sometimes hang on far beyond any possible hope of survival. In fact, the vital signs of the body may continue long after there is a

An Agony Too Deep for Words

flat brain wave. In this kind of situation or one in which debilitating pain continues unmercifully with nothing in sight but more of the same, then death becomes a welcomed relief. Death that is complete—body and mind—is better than death which refuses to terminate.

The *Christian hope* is that God in Christ has defeated this enemy too! Again Paul writes,

> Death has been swallowed up in victory.
>
> > Where, O death is your victory?
> > Where, O death is your sting?
>
> The sting of death is sin, and the power of sin is the law. But thanks be to God! He gives us the victory through our Lord Jesus Christ.[8]

God gives us complete victory ultimately, but the gift of that ultimate victory does not eliminate our present struggle. We can face our demise with great *hope* because of what is on the other side of this experience for us, but that hope does not nullify the trauma which accompanies death.

Our expectations concerning our own death or the death of one close to us may create some real problems. To think, for example, that every time a Christian faces death he will be automatically overwhelmed with a great sense *of God's peace* is just not true. What is true is that *God is with us* "in the valley of the shadow of death" whether we emotionally feel His presence or not!

Sometimes the trauma strips us of all emotional supports leaving us only with the haunting questions: *Why is this happening? Where is God?* C. S. Lewis, when he lost his wife, was plunged into the very depths of despair. In his book *A Grief Observed* he wrote:

> Meanwhile, where is God? This is one of the most disquieting symptoms. When you are happy, so happy that you have no sense of needing Him, so happy that you are tempted to feel His claims upon you as an interruption, if you remember yourself and turn to Him with gratitude and praise, you will be—or so it feels—welcomed with open arms. But go to Him when your need is desperate, when all other help is vain, and what do you find? A door slammed in your face, and a sound of bolting and double bolting on the inside. . . . What can this mean? Why is He so present a commander in our time of prosperity and so very absent a help in time of trouble?[9]

The phrase "or so it feels" explains the whole of Lewis' book. These are strong feelings flowing out of Lewis' grief and they are so encompassing that there is *no emotional room* at that moment for other feelings. Two of the last things Joy, Lewis' wife, said to him were, "you have made me happy," and "I am at peace with God." Her positive statements about her relationship with Lewis and her relationship with God did not diminish his loss.

Lewis' expectations that somehow grief would not be grief only increased his grief. He writes,

> Aren't all these notes the senseless writings of a man who won't accept the fact that there is nothing we can do with suffering except to suffer it? Who still thinks there is some device (if only he could find it) which will make pain not to be pain. It doesn't really matter whether you grip the arms of the dentist's chair or let your hands lie in your lap. The drill drills on.[10]

Regardless of what the *feelings* are (and they are not to be denied) God is with us in our moments of desperation as surely as He is with us in our moments of exhuberance.

Our emotions are not to be confused with our faith or the lack of it. Facing the awesome trauma of death will, in all likelihood, release many conflicting emotions which may be hard for both the person dying and for the person being confronted by this impending loss to understand or accept. *God's grace is greater than all our fears.*

An Agony Too Deep for Words

Lord,
Thank you for the witness of your people,
    For by their witness I know that others have
        journeyed through hard places, too,
And have found your grace to be sufficient
    when nothing else was.

Being able to see in another's story the struggle
    and the process through which he moved
Gives me perspective and hope in relation to
    my own journey.
Not that my experience will be the same,
    For no two people ever have duplicating circumstances;
Yet experiences can be similar,
    Enabling us to identify with another.

Suffering creates a common bond
    regardless of its exact nature.
Hope also engenders a deep kinship
    Among those who share it.

Lord,
Thank you that I do not live in a silent universe;
    For you have spoken to us through your Son,
        who was Himself "a man of sorrows and familiar
        with suffering."
And thank you for speaking through the lives of your
    people who believed even when they experienced the
    worst.

PART II

The Person

CHAPTER TWO

What Am I Bringing to the Struggle?

> We are not carbon copies turned out of a machine. We are not mass-produced in a factory. We are individuals with significance in history, so immensely important that no one else can live our lives or die our deaths for us. No one else can have our joys or bear our pain for us.[1]
>
> Edith Schaeffer

The most obvious answer to the question, "What am I bringing to the struggle?" is *myself.* I cannot escape *me,* try as I may, even by changing locations, jobs, spouse or whatever. My strengths and weaknesses, my hopes and fears, my blind spots, my sensitivity, my self-image, all that I am and am aspiring to be, becomes part of my resource base for dealing with the challenges and the threats that life presents. Thus, every stressful situation provides a unique opportunity for learning who I am and what is becoming of me.

Like a mirror we can see the deeper parts of ourselves reflected in the way that we respond to difficult experiences. But the image in the mirror of our experience may be greatly distorted in the initial stages of self-reflection.

Take, for instance, someone who has just lost a spouse in death. At first the feeling is that there is nothing left for which to live. "Why struggle on when the future looks so empty? How could there ever be any happiness for me without the one who has brought so much happiness to me?" These are valid feelings which need to be expressed, but they reflect only the grief of the present and not the joy of the rich memories which remain. As that individual works through his grief, he will either discover a reason for affirming life and moving on or he will resist the healing process and become bitter. In any case he has discovered something about himself. He either knows or has found an adequate base for his life or he has failed to find anything great enough to sustain him through such loss.

The other side of the coin would be someone who has lost a spouse in divorce. In this case, initial self-reflection is usually distorted by an overwhelming sense of inadequacy. The person ends up feeling like *a failure* rather than as having failed in his marriage, which of course is serious. But this latter perspective offers healthier recovery by enabling the person to deal with the real failure instead of a multitude of imagined failures.

In divorce, self-esteem is hard to maintain and the desire to run away and hide may be almost irresistible. Yet after the emotional tidal wave produced by this devastating trauma subsides, the person will have the opportunity to find out who he is after all. He can set out on a crusade to justify the marital failure, resign himself to self-pity, or discover that he can live again. The choice is his and the choice he makes is self-revealing. We must remember that to make the wrong choice does not diminish one's worth as a person, but does indicate the need for change.

Perhaps no experience that mortal man has brings such great self-disclosure as that of facing his own death. For in

What Am I Bringing to the Struggle?

actuality, we die as we have lived. If we learn to live in faith we will find it easier to die in faith. But if we live under the illusion that we have no need of God then death will be the starkest reality of our existence.

Virginia's story illustrates profoundly the strength that a genuine faith in the living God can provide. The struggle and pain were not removed, but the resources for enduring and, in the end, finding peace, flowed from her faith.

We have a biblical character in the Old Testament who is a pioneer in living through a multitude of losses. His name is Job. Without warning or explanation to him, calamity struck and continued to strike until he was stripped of everything except his faith. His friends even questioned the integrity of that faith while his wife encouraged him to give it up altogether. Yet Job entered the darkness with the kind of allegiance to God which enabled him to endure the suffering, even without understanding the *why* of it. His allegiance rested not upon some self-interest—what "goodies" can I get from God—but on the truth of God's existence and the sheer greatness and beauty of His character. Thus, he could not be driven from God, even when everything he counted dear was lost. He searched for a reason, for an answer, for a solution and received only confusing and accusing responses from his friends and silence from God.

Fortunately, the Bible gives us some insight into Job's struggle which he did not have while living through it. Satan challenged God as to the validity of Job's faith. He accused Job of believing only because of the blessings such belief brought. God knew Job and was willing to trust him to face the test.

Most of us would probably prefer less trust on God's part and more tranquility in our life style, especially if we thought His trust might usher us into the cosmic battle between good and evil. It is important for us to understand that each person is immensely significant and that what we allow God to do in us affects not only our own history but even eternity.

Job's first two losses were his possessions and his children. His response to these losses reads as follows:

> At this, Job got up and tore his robe and shaved his head. Then he fell to the ground in worship and said:
>
>> "Naked I came from my mother's womb,
>> and naked I will depart.
>
>> The Lord gave and the Lord has taken away;
>> may the name of the Lord be praised."
>
> In all this, Job did not sin by charging God with wrongdoing.[2]

To rend his coat and shave his head were expressions of enormous grief. To fall upon the ground and to worship God revealed incredible faith in the God he had come to know. *What a man!*—which is exactly what God had said to Satan. Again, what we carry with us into our struggles is most determinative in how we deal with those struggles. Thus to approach life with only humanistic beliefs,* makes about as much sense as playing Russian roulette with all the chambers of the gun loaded.

Job clung to his faith through the first tests, but Satan was not finished with him yet:

---

* Humanism is the philosophy that man can start from himself alone and create his own universals, his own values and his own meaning for life apart from God. Such a view ultimately ends in despair, because no matter how far you project it, you never come to an absolute. When man is made to be the center of all things instead of God you are left with an uncertain and distorted view of reality. "A finite point unless it has an infinite reference point is absurd." (Sartre) The strange phenomenon of our day is that humanism, which starts out making man to be everything, has ended up making man to be nothing more than a part of the cosmic machine locked in determinism.

What Am I Bringing to the Struggle?

> "Skin for skin!" Satan replied. "A man will give all he has for his own life. But stretch out your hand and strike his flesh and bones, and he will surely curse you to your face."
>
> The Lord said to Satan, "Very well, then, he is in your hands; but you must spare his life."[3]

The cosmic battle continued as Job was afflicted with painful sores from the soles of his feet to the top of his head. His wife, out of her frustration, chided him, " 'Are you still holding on to your integrity? Curse God and die!' He replied, 'You are talking like a foolish woman. Shall we accept good from God, and not trouble?' "[4]

In the midst of all this Job's well-meaning friends came to comfort him, but instead they ended up accusing him of bringing his misfortune upon himself. One friend made the following observation, " 'As I have observed, those who plow evil and those who sow trouble reap it.' "[5]

Another added:

> Does the Almighty pervert what is right?
> When your children sinned against him,
>   he gave them over to the penalty of their sin.
> But if you will look to God
>   and plead with the Almighty,
> if you are pure and upright,
>   even now he will rouse himself on your behalf
>   and restore you to your rightful place.[6]

A third comforter said:

> Yet if you devote your heart to him
>   and stretch out your hands to him,
> if you put away the sin that is in your hand
>   and allow no evil to dwell in your tent,
> then you will lift up your face without shame;
>   you will stand firm and without fear.[7]

From their limited perspective that all suffering comes because of one's personal sin, Job's friends found it easier to criticize and judge him than to understand and love him.

Job became discouraged and depressed as they spoke to him. Depression often comes with physical and emotional pain. His agony was so severe that he wished he had never been born. Non-existence seemed better to him than existence, if existing meant suffering of this magnitude.

Job complained plenty about his plight; he was not a silent sufferer. We need to remember that to trust God does not eliminate our humanity, but it enables us to move through our bitterness into hope. Perhaps a list of some of Job's complaints would help us to realize that someone else has felt some of the same things we feel at times. Job complained of

> *the loss of meaning:* "... Let me alone; my days have no meaning ... I have no peace, no quietness; I have no rest, but only turmoil."[3]
>
> *the feeling of futility:* "One man dies in full vigor, completely secure and at ease, his body well nourished ... Another man dies in bitterness of soul, never having enjoyed anything good. Side by side they lie in the dust..."[9]
>
> *the undeserved calamity:* "... What have I done to you, O watcher of men?"[10]
>
> *the lack of dependability:* "... My brothers are as undependable as intermittent streams ..."[11]
>
> *the loss of sleep:* "When I lie down I think, 'How long before I get up?' The night drags on and I toss till dawn."[12]
>
> *the loss of joy:* "My days are swifter than a runner; they fly away without a glimpse of joy."[13]
>
> *the loss of status:* "I have become a laughingstock to my

What Am I Bringing to the Struggle?

> friends... men at ease have contempt for misfortune..."[14]
>
> *the anguish of not being understood:* "I have heard many things like these; miserable comforters are you all! Will your long-winded speeches never end?... I could speak like you, if you were in my place. If only you would be altogether silent! For you, that would be wisdom."[15]
>
> *the unending problems:* "Man born of woman is of few days and full of trouble."[16]
>
> *the lack of justice:* "Though I cry, 'I've been wronged!' I get no response; though I call for help, there is no justice."[17]
>
> *the loss of support:* "My kinsmen have gone away; my friends have forgotten me."[18]
>
> *the prosperity of the wicked:* "Why do the wicked live on, growing old and increasing in power?"[19]
>
> *the inability to find God:* "If only I knew where to find him... But if I go to the east, he is not there; if I go to the west, I do not find him. Where is he at work in the north, I do not see him; when he turns to the south, I catch no glimpse of him."[20]

God had not abandoned Job, but had entrusted him with the severest of tests. Job was human. He complained; he despaired. Still in the midst of it all, he cried out, "Though he slay me, yet will I trust in Him."[21] That is authentic faith, the kind that transcends the pain or the pleasure of the moment and enables one to know God intimately.

God's response to Job's question of *why* and to his complaints of anguish was not to give him an abstract, conceptual answer but rather to reveal Himself to Job. Anyone who has never experienced the incomprehensible greatness of the presence of God in the midst of dire circumstances might wonder how this could be an answer.

Job found his encounter with God to be of infinitely greater value than having his trauma explained. To come to know that we can trust in the character of God beyond what we can understand and that He is with us even in our suffering brings more hope than could any explanation.

What Job saw when God revealed Himself was not a physical image, but rather the greatness and love of the infinite, personal God displayed in His mighty acts of creation. Job declared:

> Surely I spoke of things I did not understand,
> things too wonderful for me to know . . .
> My ears had heard of you
>   but now my eyes have seen you.[22]

There is no other way for finite men to know the infinite God other than through His self-disclosure. God's greatest act of personal unveiling came when He broke into history as the God-man in Jesus Christ. To take seriously God's revelation of Himself in Christ is to know assuredly that His love for us is immeasurable and that we can trust Him even when we do not understand Him.

Another word is needed as we wrestle with the mystery of suffering. It is true that we reap what we sow. If we pursue such things as faith, hope, love, we will experience a richness in life concomitant with that pursuit. If we live recklessly and sow to the wind, the Bible declares that we will reap the whirlwind. The investments we make with our lives multiply accordingly.

Keep in mind the perspective that not all misfortune comes because of individual sin. It did not with Job; his was a part of the cosmic battle between God and Satan. Added to this is the reality that we live in an abnormal world. The Fall spoken of in the Scriptures is not a

What Am I Bringing to the Struggle? 47

religious theory but an obvious fact. All of creation, including man, has been affected by the Fall and will continue to be affected until God brings history to a conclusion. This does not mean that there is no beauty to be enjoyed in the world, but it does mean there is no perfection within creation or within man. Still life can be affirmed and enjoyed and we can have a positive impact in the affairs of men. Francis Bacon said in 1620:

> Man by the Fall fell at the same time from his state of innocence and from his dominion over creation. Both of these losses, however, can even in this life be in some parts repaired; the former by religion and faith, the latter by the arts and sciences.[23]

There is good news for you if you find yourself struggling either for personal meaning or with some catastrophic dilemma. God exists and He longs to be involved in a personal way in your experience. If you are willing to let Him be God in your life, would you simply pray and invite the Living Christ to come into your life and to make any and all changes needed. Ask Him to forgive your sin and to fill you with His Spirit. Thank Him for coming in and trust Him in the process of growth which must follow. Find a Bible and begin reading John's gospel as you seek to better understand Him and what your commitment means.

If you have already made a start with Him, why not reaffirm that commitment and ask Him to quiet your spirit and to begin, in whatever way He chooses, to make Himself known to you in the area that you need Him most.

What Am I Bringing to the Struggle

Lord,
Thank you that I matter greatly to you,
    that my life with all its joy and pain
    has eternal significance.

Thank you for the gift of authentic freedom
    which prevents either outward pressures or
    inner urges from completely determining
    what becomes of me.
Even though I cannot always control my circumstances
    I still have some choice about my response to them.

Thank you that, although everything which happens
    to me is not good,
You are working for my good in all things.

Thank you that when I do not understand what is
    happening and cry out in fear or anger,
You do not abandon me,
    But rather move with me through the anguish
    enabling me to trust you beyond any finite
    knowledge I possess.

Lord,
Give me the courage to walk with you and to love you
    no matter what!

PART III

The Process

LORD, IF I EVER NEEDED YOU, IT'S NOW!

Answer me when I call to you,
    O my righteous God.
Give me relief from my distress;
    be merciful to me and hear my prayer.
Give ear to my words, O Lord,
    consider my sighing.
Listen to my cry for help,
    my King and my God,
    for to you I pray.
Be merciful to me, Lord, for I am faint;
    O Lord, heal me, for my bones are in agony.
My soul is in anguish.
    How long, O Lord, how long?
I am worn out from groaning;
    all night long I flood my bed with weeping
    and drench my couch with tears.
Hear my voice when I call, O Lord;
    be merciful to me and answer me . . .
Do not hide your face from me . . .
Do not reject me or forsake me,
    O God my Savior,
Though my father and mother forsake me,
    the Lord will receive me.
Teach me your way, O Lord;
    lead me in a straight path . . .
I am still confident of this:
    I will see the goodness of the Lord
    in the land of the living.
Wait for the Lord;
    be strong and take heart
    and wait for the Lord.

        —From Psalms 4:1; 5:1-2; 6:2-3, 6; 27:7,
        9-11, 13-14

CHAPTER THREE

Let the Heart Speak

Questions which spring out of our difficult situations can become the avenue to a more intimate relationship with God. The writer of Psalm 10 began with the questions, "Why, O Lord, do you stand far off? Why do you hide yourself in times of trouble?"

It always *seems* to us that the presence of trouble means the absence of God and the presence of God surely must mean the absence of trouble. But this is not the case. God is with us, but His presence does not inhibit our freedom nor does it remove us from all the suffering common to mankind. Remember, the Scriptures make clear the fact that we do live in an abnormal world because of the Fall. We can be grateful that God's protection spares us from experiencing much that could go wrong even though He chooses not to spare us everything.

The beauty that we have seen, the good that we have experienced and the greatness that we have contemplated are gifts from a benevolent Father who delights in giving superb gifts to His children. One of these exceptional gifts is the significance given to man. Even in the Fall God refused to make Adam or his choice less potent than the act of one created in His own image (Genesis 3). This means that neither has our significance been reduced, because we are descendants of Adam. Adam's choice allowed evil to enter the world, and it is that evil against which we struggle even now. The good news is that we are not alone in our struggle and that a day is coming when "He will wipe every tear from our eyes. There will be no more death or mourning or crying or pain . . ."[1] The future is exceedingly bright for the people of God! Sometimes our distress may be so great that holding on to God's promise regarding the future may be the only hope which can keep us going.

Faith's first step toward release is honesty with ourselves and with God about what is going on inside us. Refusal to deal realistically with our feelings can leave a root of bitterness which may become an inner wedge between ourselves and God. If God loves us as the Scriptures affirm, He certainly will not abandon us even when our pain squeezes negative responses from us.

Again, C. S. Lewis, who was a modern day hero of the faith wrote out of the agony of his grief:

> Not that I am (I think) in much danger of ceasing to believe in God. The real danger is of coming to believe such dreadful things about Him. . . . What chokes every prayer and every hope is the memory of all the prayers H. and I offered and all the false hopes we had. Not hopes raised merely by our own wishful thinking; hopes encouraged, even forced upon us, by false diagnosis, by X-ray photographs, by strange remissions, by one temporary recovery that might have ranked as a miracle. Step by step we were 'led up the garden path.' Time after time, when He seemed most gracious He was really preparing the next torture.[2]

This does not sound like the Lewis of faith we have envisioned, but it is precisely that *Lewis who believed enough* to honestly express the thoughts and feelings his pain created. The next morning he wrote in his notes, "I wrote that last night. It was a yell rather than a thought."[3] Out of his pain Lewis discovered that God can endure our yells.

We must trust God enough to speak the absolute truth rising from the inner depths of our being. Only in so doing can we open the door for his healing grace to enter.

Let the Heart Speak

Lord,
Can I tell you how I really feel
　or must I only utter what others expect
　from one who believes?
　　Does faith make one less human?
Do I dare believe that you are truly my Father
　and I your child?
　　Would not such belief demand transparency?
Does Christianity rest on an illusion
　that life is always explainable, beautiful and easy
　for those who follow you?
　　Or does it rest on One who Himself bore a
　　　cross on our behalf?

The longing for life without pain is strong
　within me.
　　But so is the hope that for those who walk
　　　with you, the best is yet to be!

My fear inhibits me; your love releases me.
　Release me now, O God, that I may praise
　　your name.

CHAPTER FOUR

There Must Be Some Mistake

To be confronted with unexpected circumstances which bring more pain—physical and/or emotional—than we are prepared to take in, leaves us in utter shock. We may walk around in a daze feeling as if there were an invisible wall separating us from the world. Nothing seems real. What others say to us fails to register. It is as if some great meteor landed squarely on top of us, totally demolishing us for the moment. We are disoriented and disinterested.

What we need is *time*; time to assimilate what is transpiring; time for some of the numbness to pass; time to regroup enough to face the truth and to mobilize whatever resources we have for dealing with it. The importance of this time-buffer must not be underestimated or overlooked.

When Job's friends heard of his troubles they went at once to comfort him:

> "When they saw him from a distance, they could hardly recognize him; they began to weep aloud, and they tore their robes and sprinkled dust on their heads [an outward expression of inner grief]. Then they sat on the ground with him for

seven days and seven nights. No one said a word to him, because they saw how great his suffering was."[1]

They, too, were shocked and recognized that Job was in no condition to begin any kind of conversation about the tragedies which had occurred.

While in shock our minds are not capable of fully grasping the reality thrust upon us. But patience and understanding will help us to bring our situation into focus more quickly and enable us to begin to move out of such total disorientation.

Caring friends who will move with us in the healing process are truly a special gift from the Lord.

There Must Be Some Mistake

Lord, Not Me! Not Me!
> There must be some mistake.
>> How could such a thing be?
>
> Reassure me that it's all a dream;
>> That I will awaken and all will be well again.
>
> What is the meaning of this numbness, this emptiness?
>> Why do I feel so detached from everything?
>
> Lord, It is hard to face the truth
>> when the truth carries such pain.
>
> Be thou greater than the pain!

CHAPTER FIVE

Why Me?

The more intense a person's struggle, the more one is driven to seek the *why* of it. Two things appear immediately in this quest for the cause. One is, to believe in God as a Loving Father is to cease to believe in a random universe. Everything must have some meaning or purpose; nothing can be accepted as inane. It is not blind fate which guides the destinies of men. The other thing which soon becomes apparent is the inequality of suffering in the human community. Living for some is a much greater struggle than for others. Why? That is the question which annoys us repeatedly in our pilgrimage.

The weight of the biblical message in regard to pain and suffering is not in the direction of *cause* but of *response*. We certainly have plenty of general indications concerning causes, such as man's freedom, the Fall and Satan's attacks, but the *why* of specific suffering for any of us remains an unanswerable mystery. Philip Yancey, in his book *Where Is God When It Hurts,* points out clearly that the real issue in suffering is not *who* caused it but what will be *my response.*

An important part of our response to the difficulty facing us is to deal realistically with the strong emotions generated by that difficulty. The Psalmist knew this quite well and wrote:

Out of the depths I cry to you, O Lord;
   O Lord, hear my voice.
Let your ears be attentive
   to my cry for mercy.[1]

Why, O Lord, do you stand far off?
   Why do you hide yourself in times of trouble?[2]

How long, O Lord? Will you forget me forever?
   How long will you hide your face from me?
How long must I wrestle with my thoughts
   and every day have sorrow in my heart?
How long will my enemy triumph over me?[3]

O Lord, do not rebuke me in your anger
   or discipline me in your wrath.
Be merciful to me, Lord, for I am faint;
   O Lord, heal me, for my bones are in agony.
My soul is in anguish.
   How long, O Lord, how long? . . .

I am worn out from groaning;
   all night long I flood my bed with weeping
   and drench my couch with tears.
My eyes grow weak with sorrow;
   they fail because of all my foes.[4]

John Claypool, in his book *Tracks Of A Fellow Struggler,* points out that the classic forms that temptation always takes are presumption and despair. The first of these is one's getting so frustrated with God that he takes

Why Me?

things in his own hands and explodes in some fit of rage. The second is to give up altogether and dissolve into despair. He writes of his own experience with his daughter's leukemia:

> I experienced both forms of temptation in a most acute way. My presumptive temptation was to get angry and rebellious toward God and thus "overheat" my spirit. As I watched my little daughter suffer, I could see no reason or purpose in what was happening to her. The flow of events did not seem to be going in any meaningful direction, and I had my moments when I understood how a man could raise his fist to heaven and curse God. At times I was not far from looking up and shouting: "Just what on earth do you think you are doing in all of this anyway?" At other times the temptation to despair was very near, when I felt like saying: "I quit. I give up. I can't stand it any longer. Stop the world. I want to get off."
>
> Yes, both of these temptations loomed large on the horizon as I stood there helpless in the darkness, but I am here to report that I did not succumb to either one. Why? Because down there at the bottom—this promise of Isaiah came true! I was given the gift of patience, the gift of enduring. I was given the strength "to walk and not faint."[5]

The promise he spoke of is found in Isaiah 40:31:

> But those who hope in the Lord
>   will renew their strength.
> They will soar on wings like eagles;
>   they will run and not grow weary,
>   they will walk and not be faint.

John at that moment could not soar or run, but he found by God's grace that he could keep on walking through this shadow which was all encompassing as his little daughter lay close to death.

The Psalmist, too, refuses to give up his belief in the goodness of God even in the midst of his despair. Such belief does not keep the angry feelings from flooding our soul, but it can keep those feelings from continuing as the dominant ones:

> But I trust in your unfailing love;
>   my heart rejoices in your salvation.
> I will sing to the Lord,
>   for he has been good to me.[6]

The strongest emotion which the "Why me?" cry squeezes from us is anger, anger that comes from our fear. And the tap root of our fear is a *perceived threat to our survival*. That perceived threat may be very real, as it was in the case of John Claypool: ". . . . on a Saturday evening, with the snow falling softly outside the window, Laura Lue died in her own bed, in her own room."[7]

In dealing with this tragedy John shares that he "looked down three alternative roads that seemed to lead out of this darkness." Two appeared to be dead ends: the road of unquestioning resignation and the road of total intellectual understanding. The road which offered the most hope was the one which came out of his faith and he identifies it as "the road of gratitude." When life is seen as a gift, received and participated in with the open hands of gratitude, then joy can return as the loss is accepted.

We may identify our fear as the fear of pain itself; the fear that this thing will alter our lives to the extent that nothing will ever be the same again; the fear that we may not be able to cope with the situation or accept it; the fear of failure; the fear of losing control and of becoming dependent; the fear of losing our self-respect and/or the respect of others; the fear of losing our place or our power or our worth; or the fear that all delight in life will be lost forever.

Fear usually creates a tremendous amount of self-doubt and guilt. The question, *"What is wrong with me that I would be thinking and feeling this way?"* can loom over us like a giant weight prepared to crush the life from us.

It can help us immensely to realize that an angry person is a fearful person. Our anger can subside as we identify our fear and open it up to the God who is present with us "in the time of trouble," even if we do not emotionally perceive His presence.

Listen to a young mother as she wrote out her plea for God to intervene in helping her overcome fear:

I'm afraid.
   Why, I'm not sure.
   Of what, I'm not sure.
But, I'm afraid.

For a long time I could handle this fear—
   with a mask
   or a good cry
   or a prayer of panic
   or a physical moving away from
     the cause of my fear.

But I can no longer handle it.
It's beginning to handle me.
   And that frightens me.

I've tried everything I know,
But it seems I've just used everything up.
   I've tried reasoning with myself that

my fears are ungrounded.
 I've tried telling myself that I'm really
  okay.
It hurts to be fearful like this
And it causes me to miss out on so much
  of life.
 I'm afraid to think, to feel, to reach out.
 I'm afraid to be what I am
  and afraid to change.
"Life is a gift", he keeps telling me.
 Why do I feel that I have to earn it?
"No mistake is fatal," he says.
 So why am I convinced mine are?

Dear Lord, I've tried turning this all over
 to you
But there's something in the way.
 I guess my faith is too small.
 I'm sorry.

I've believed in you since I was a little girl
And I've always known you love me
 But somewhere I picked up the idea
  that I have to solve my own problems
  — right my own mistakes
  — settle my own nerves
  that you are standing by loving and
   caring and helping from time to time
 Yet expecting me to stand on my own
  two feet . . .
   My feet are shaky
   And I'm tired.
  Tired of trying to figure out what's
   expected of me—then trying to do it;

Why Me?

Tired of that instant fear and the
   feeling I get across the back of my neck
   when I think I have made a mistake;
Tired of explaining myself to everyone
   so they'll think I'm O.K.;
Tired of fighting life.

Lord, looking back,
You have done a lot for me.
You gave me hope when I didn't care
   whether I lived or not.
You gave me a deep love for my
   family and a real joy in
   being a wife and a mother.
You gave me strength when my
   children were seriously ill.
You gave me your hand when I
   couldn't find the way.

But, dear Father, today I hurt.
I don't know why I can't trust you more.
I don't know why I can't accept life as
   a gift and quit feeling like I have
   to earn my right to live.
I'm sorry Lord, that I keep trying to be
   my own God.

Dear Lord, can you answer my "why's"?
Can you handle my fears?
Can you calm my nerves so
   that they don't overcome me?
Can you change something inside of me
   so that I can really live again?

I'm sorry Lord.
But I don't know anything else to do.

Please take what little faith I have
  at this moment—
    and begin to work in me now.
  No matter what the cost.
Lord, I hurt.

Today she is free of that overpowering fear and part of the reason, she believes, is finally being able to identify and acknowledge her fear by opening it up to God and to another person who helped make God more real to her.

We may not be able to change immediately, or perhaps ever, the thing which has caused us to cry "Why Me?" but we do have a choice about our response—we can pull into our shell and become bitter or we can push on with whatever help is available into the very light of God's love.

Why Me?

Lord,
Why me?
   What have I done?
All around me life goes on with such pleasantness;
   Others enjoying themselves while I live in
      misery.
Is there no justice?
   Surely there is a reason, but what?
My anger spreads in all directions;
   Everywhere I look I find grievances.
Others seem to avoid me like a plague.
   My fear has isolated me.

Lord,
Forbid that this bitterness should take permanent root in me; Let it be but a shadow through which I move toward the greater light of your love.

CHAPTER SIX

Promises

For those of us who believe that God is, it is quite natural that we try every means available to get Him to help make everything all right again when we are in a difficult place. Others who never thought seriously about God one way or another usually do so when the going gets tough enough. All men are finite and as such are driven to seek the Infinite when there is a serious threat to their survival—physically, emotionally, relationally, economically or in any other area that is of importance to that individual. Being driven to seek God out of dire circumstances is not to be frowned upon by anyone. That is a healthy response to the reality of man's finiteness—man is not a god and was never intended to live apart from the One who created him. Our stubborn pride may cause us to stand aloof from faith in the infinite personal God even when our need for that faith is painfully obvious. It makes no sense to resist the greatest source of help man has, especially when the circumstances of his life have crushed every illusion that he is self-sufficient.

However, it is certainly not necessary to wait for dire circumstances in order to turn to the Lord. As one hears the message of Christ, he will, *we hope,* respond to the truth of God's love as the Father draws him to it. If not, then by all means he should look in God's direction when the needs are great!

The Scriptures encourage us to make our needs known to the Lord, "Do not be anxious about anything, but in everything, by prayer and petition, with thanksgiving, present your requests to God. And the peace of God, which transcends all understanding, will guard your hearts and your minds in Christ Jesus."[1] Prayer is our most valuable resource! Speaking from the depth of our being to God about our needs and listening to Him through the Scriptures and through our experiences with Him, can be the avenue by which He gives us sufficient resources for dealing with our situation.

God's love for us is real but so is the fact that we live in an abnormal world. We must accept the reality that everything is not always going to turn out the way we want it. Yet we do have an important promise to which we can cling: "And we know that in all things God works for the good of those who love him, who have been called according to his purpose."[2] The promise is not that everything that happens to us will be good in and of itself, but that God is at work even in our most miserable circumstances to bring good out of them. Without this hope, great would be the waste of a large part of human experience.

It may take a long time to ever recognize anything positive coming out of a devastating situation, but too many people have given witness to this fact for us to dismiss it as wishful thinking. Joni Eareckson[3] is one of those witnesses. She broke her neck in a diving accident in 1967 and has been paralyzed since. There was a time when she desperately wanted to die. Now she says of her accident:

> Few of us have the luxury—it took me forever to think of it as that—to come to ground zero with God. Before the accident, my questions had always been, "How will God fit into this situation? How will He affect my dating life? My career plans? The things I enjoy?" All those options were gone. It was me, just a helpless body, and God.
>
> I had no other identity but God, and gradually He became enough. I became overwhelmed with the phenomenon of the personal God, who created the universe, living in my life. He would make me attractive and worthwhile—I could not do it without Him.
>
> The first months, even years, I was consumed with the unanswered questions of what God was trying to teach me. I probably secretly hoped that by figuring out God's ideas, I could learn my lesson and then He would heal me.
>
> I guess every Christian with an experience similar to mine goes back to the Book of Job for answers. Here was a righteous man who suffered more than I could imagine. Everything was taken away from him. Strangely, the Book of Job does not answer any questions about why God let the tragedies happen. But Job clung to God, and God rewarded him.
>
> 'Is that what God wants?' I wondered. My focus changed from demanding an explanation from God to humbly depending on Him.
>
> Okay, I am paralyzed. It's terrible. I don't like it. But can God still use me, paralyzed? Can I, paralyzed, still worship God and love Him? He has taught me that I can.
>
> Maybe God's gift to me is my dependence on Him. I will never reach the place where I'm self-sufficient, where God is crowded out of my life. I'm aware of His grace to me every

moment. My need for help is obvious every day when I wake up, flat on my back, waiting for someone to come dress me. I can't even comb my hair or blow my nose alone!

But I have friends who care. I have the beauty of the scenery. With my art sales, I can even support myself financially—the dream of a handicapped person.

The peace that counts is an internal peace, and God has lavished me with that peace.

And there's one more thing. I have hope for the future. The Bible speaks of our bodies being 'glorified' in heaven. In high school that was always a hazy, foreign concept. But now I realize that I will be healed. I haven't been cheated out of being a complete person—I'm just going through a forty-year delay, and God is with me even through that.

Being 'glorified'—I know the meaning of that now. It's the time, after my death here, when I'll be on my feet dancing.[4]

What can you say to such witness except that Joni is one remarkable human being who has discovered the incredible truth about the greatness of God's love and care for us! He is at work in all things for our good.

In the midst of our own struggle, before anything about it makes much sense, we will in all probability attempt to bargain with God. We would like for Him to undo or redo our circumstances; to lessen or, better yet, to eliminate the problem. We may even make many promises to Him. There is nothing wrong with this, but we must remember: although He is at work for our good, His work may not eliminate the bad through which we are having to walk. The real question is, "Am I willing to trust Him even when He's not doing it my way?"

Promises

Lord,
I know that you take no pleasure in the suffering
  of your people.
    You desire only the best for us.
What possible good could come from allowing this
  to continue?
    Surely you are as ready for this to pass as I.
You promised never to leave us nor forsake us;
  your presence must lessen the struggle, mustn't it?
Maybe I have not been as true to you as I should,
  but I am really ready to get on with serving you
  now.
This experience has taught me some things I needed
  to know;
    Give me the chance to use what I've learned.
Lord,
Should you choose to intervene in such a way as to
  give me immediate relief,
    Let me never forget your goodness to me.
Should you choose not to intervene but rather to walk
  with me through the shadow,
    Give me the grace to know you are there!

CHAPTER SEVEN

What's the Use?

In the midst of struggle, when nothing seems to be working to bring relief, most will experience a degree of depression. It comes when the feeling exists that there is nothing left to do that will make any difference. Having been unable to find a remedy for this intolerable situation opens the door for despair to enter. The more intense and serious the "unsolvable" problem is, the greater the possibility for despondency.

We are not dealing here primarily with mood swings, which every human being experiences to some degree. However it may help to look briefly at the occasional "down" feelings common to us all. Our mood swings are related to our personality and to the way we deal with life. There are a multitude of potential catalysts for a downward swing, such as lack of rest or an inadequate diet; unresolved conflict or repressed emotions; false guilt coming from an over-sensitive conscience or true guilt coming from the violation of one's inner value system; the completion of a strenuous task, or reaching a long sought after goal. We can expend ourselves emotionally and feel as though we have nothing left. Perhaps this was the problem of Sir Winston Churchill, who, although a tower of strength for England during the War, was personally given to serious bouts of depression.

Many of the world's geniuses have been plagued with the problem of despondency. Edgar Allen Poe, after writing the short story "The Pit and the Pendulum," plunged into deep depression. And, according to Kenneth Hildebrand:

> Sydney J. Harris, syndicated columnist, ... reports that nothing seems to account for his moods; they just come. Since he has learned this, he anticipates them and does not let them upset him. He sits them out quietly and thus "cancels the harm they can do." He confesses that sometimes in the depth of a low mood he thinks his writing is so poor that he hopes the editor will throw it in the waste basket. "Actually," he adds, "the columns I knock out when I am feeling bad are often better than the ones I write in a good mood." He concludes that a depressed person cannot judge his own work accurately.[1]

Tim LaHaye reminds us that "During a low mood, things that ordinarily are absorbed and cause no emotional distress suddenly become a source of irritation that brings on depression."[2]

Take note of your own mood-swing patterns. Try to identify what they are related to and how you are dealing with the low swings. You may be surprised to find that without conscious thought you have learned how to move through them without great discomfort. Or you may discover a more serious, chronic problem of depression which could stem all the way from continual over-exhaustion of your energies to that of an organic malfunction. Depending on the cause, you may simply need to rest or, perhaps as Sydney Harris has learned, to anticipate your low mood and not let it upset you, having learned from experience that it will pass shortly.

If you have violated the law of your conscience you will need to deal with that directly and not repress it. At this point it becomes extremely important that we understand the Scriptures sufficiently to make a distinction between false or unfounded guilt and true guilt. For example, we experience false guilt when we see ourselves as being responsible for everyone else's happiness and feel guilty when they are not happy. Recognizing the trap we have allowed ourselves to fall into and deliberately changing our view with regard to this situation can alleviate our guilt feelings. On the other hand, if we are truly guilty of violating one of God's laws and have failed to live and relate as we should, then the biblical call is to *repentance*—acknowledge our wrong, seek God's forgiveness and make restitution whenever it is possible to do so. A clear conscience which comes from being right with God and others is an incredible release that usually swings our mood upward with great force.

David, after his great sin, wrote,

Blessed is he
   whose transgressions are forgiven,
   whose sins are covered.
Blessed is the man
   whose sin the Lord does not count against him
   and in whose spirit is no deceit.

When I kept silent,
   my bones wasted away
   through my groaning all day long.
For day and night
   your hand was heavy upon me;
my strength was sapped

> as in the heat of summer.
> Then I acknowledged my sin to you
> and did not cover up my iniquity.
>
> I said, "I will confess
> my transgressions to the Lord"—
> And you forgave
> the guilt of my sin . . .
>
> Rejoice in the Lord and be glad . . .[3]

God offers us forgiveness and the resources for beginning again. One of those important resources is the capacity to forgive ourselves. If we asked God to forgive us and the guilt lingers, then we need to ask Him to help us forgive ourselves, because He has already done so. The problem lies with our own unforgiving spirit at that point.

Should chronic depression persist, let me suggest that a physician or a competent counselor, or both, be consulted in order to help you find the root problem and gain some relief.

The kind of depression we are most concerned with in this section on *process* is that which can come as we struggle with difficult situations in life.

Job, as we discussed in the second chapter, experienced tremendous losses which threw him into deep depression. He was so despondent that he wished he had never been born. Looking at his losses and his description of how he felt about each can help us understand why the Scriptures say, "No temptation has seized you except what is common to man."[4] Someone else has been there before us. No one else's experience will be exactly like ours in all details because we are unique. Yet others have felt the pain of loss and have been tempted to cry out against God in presumption or give up in despair.

What's the Use?

C. S. Lewis shares with us the paralyzing effect which depression, born of his grief, had on him:

> No one ever told me about the laziness of grief. Except at my job—where the machine seems to run on much as usual—I loathe the slightest effort. Not only writing but even reading a letter is too much. Even shaving. What does it matter now whether my cheek is rough or smooth? ... I once read the sentence "I lay awake all night with toothache, thinking about toothache and about lying awake." That's true to life. Part of every misery is, so to speak, the misery's shadow or reflection: the fact that you don't merely suffer but have to keep on thinking about the fact that you suffer. I not only live each endless day in grief, but live each day thinking about living each day in grief.[5]

David, the man after God's own heart, was very human as we have already noticed. He knew what it was to be depressed and what his best resource for dealing with it was.

> Give ear to my words, O Lord,
>   consider my sighing.
> Listen to my cry for help,
>   my King and my God
>   for to you I pray.[6]

Sighing (periodically taking a deep audible breath) is a sure sign of weariness and despondency. David in his "sighing" cried out to the One he believed could help as no other.

Another song of the Psalmist states it clearly:

> Why are you downcast, O my soul?
>   Why so disturbed within me?
> Put your hope in God,
>   for I will yet praise him,

> my Savior and my God.
>
> My soul is downcast within me;
> > therefore I will remember you
>
> from the land of the Jordan,
> > the heights of Hermon—from Mount Mizar.
>
> Deep calls to deep
> > in the roar of your waterfalls;
>
> all your waves and breakers
> > have swept over me.[7]

The writer is downcast but he clings to the hope that he has known in the Lord. He *recalls God's care for him* in the past and that gives him the needed assurance that God can be trusted in his present situation. Men of faith all through the ages have found comfort and the courage to go on by remembering God's faithfulness to them. "Deep calls to deep" out of the mystery of life and those who have responded to that call by faith have changed the course of history.

The Lord has given us an incredible promise that we can count on even if our feelings betray our faith at the moment: "And God is faithful; he will not let you be tempted beyond what you can bear. But when you are tempted, he will also provide a way out so that you can stand up under it."[8]

The journey from despair to faith may be a long, difficult one at times but we do not need to make it alone. Ask the Lord, if only out of raw faith, to help you push through the shadow into the very light of His love beyond.

What's the Use?

Lord,
What's the use?
  Why should I go on?

Day and night this darkness hangs over me,
  like storm clouds that cover the sun.

The clouds are so black they obscure everything.
  Will the sun ever shine for me again?

Today life holds no pleasure for me.
  All joy has vanished.

Loneliness and despair refuse to leave me.
  A sense of hopelessness overwhelms me.

The feeling of being trapped in an intolerable
  situation lingers on without relief–
  the victim of things now out of control.

My mind refuses to release the dismal thoughts
  which preoccupy it.
  Everything becomes an excuse for worry.

Forsake me not, O Lord, during the dark night
  of my soul.
    Let me know that this too shall pass.
  Make me to hear joy and gladness again!

CHAPTER EIGHT

Acceptance

Acceptance of life's hard places is one of God's most profound gifts to us humans. With a disposition prone to rebellion and an insatiable attraction to the "easy" life, our "normal" reaction to threat is to kick and scream. We want immediate relief or, better yet, not even the possibility of pain.

A television special was made of Jo Roman's deciding to practice her theory of "rational suicide" when she discovered that she had cancer. She went off alone for three months without allowing her family or friends access to that decision-making process. Then she called them together and announced what she had chosen to do. What she gave was a "rationalization," not a valid reason, for taking her own life. One of her statements was, "Why should I experience one minute's pain should I choose not to?"

Pain and the fear of losing control are very great for all of us, yet taking our own lives as a way of eliminating the fear and avoiding the pain also eliminates the creative possibilities for perhaps God's deepest work in our lives. Healing, or at least remission, is not an absolute impossibility. What we and those who love us may learn in our struggle to survive may bring us closer to understanding the very essence of our existence. Man cannot live without pain, physical and emotional. Jo Roman had a daughter. She could not have brought that daughter into the world without some pain. The obvious love between mother and daughter would no doubt mean that what Jo had experienced with her daughter was well worth the pain.

To accept what we cannot change, to turn loose of what we cannot keep are the only options we have which keep life from running aground.

Elisbeth Elliot lost her missionary husband in an Auca Indian massacre on January 8, 1956. In order to share the message of Christ, she, along with her small daughter and the sister of another one of the slain missionaries, went into the very village of the tribesmen who had killed their husband and brother. After reading Catherine Marshall's book *To Live Again* Elisbeth Elliot wrote her a letter expressing her gratitude for the book. In the letter she also wrote, "It is possible for us to lose our lives any day. The Aucas are still savages, who do not even think of killing as wrong. Fear can drive them to kill in a twinkling. What the future holds for Rachel and Valerie and me is God's business."[1] She went on to write, "Your solution to grief is just another way of giving the same answer that God gave me in the first empty days—accept this. Only in acceptance lies peace—not in forgetting nor in resignation nor in busy-ness."[2]

Resignation is surrender to fate. Acceptance is surrender to God. Resignation lies down quietly in an empty universe. Acceptance rises up to meet the God who fills that universe with purpose and destiny. Resignation says, "I can't." Acceptance says, "God can!" Resignation paralyzes the life process. Acceptance releases the process for its greatest creativity. Resignation says, "It's all over for me." Acceptance asks, "Now that I am here, what's next, Lord?" Resignation says, "What a waste." Acceptance asks, "In what redemptive way will you use this mess, Lord?" Resignation says, "I am alone." Acceptance says, "I belong to you, O God!"

Authentic Christian faith is different from simply believing that this or that can happen if one only believes without a single doubt. The object of genuine faith is the unseen God who created all things and who came to us personally in Jesus of Nazereth. To actively and passionately commit the whole of our lives to God-in-Christ is the biblical faith which saves.

A demanding spirit can prevent the grace of God from enabling us to reach that emotional and spiritual solace called acceptance. This is why Christ said, "Let the little children come to me, and do not hinder them, for the kingdom of God belongs to such as these. I tell you the truth, anyone who will not receive the kingdom of God like a little child will never enter it."[3] The picture is that of simple trust and willing obedience, with spontaneity and openness abounding.

Peter Marshall gives us another picture of a negative characteristic all too common among those of us who identify ourselves as God's children:

> Suppose a child has a broken toy.
> He brings the toy to his father, saying that he himself has tried to fix it and has failed.
> He asks his father to do it for him.
>
> The father gladly agrees . . . takes the toy . . .
> And begins to work.
>
> Now obviously the father can do his work most quickly and easily if the child makes no attempt to interfere, simply sits

> quietly watching, or even goes about other business, with never a doubt that the toy is being successfully mended.
>
> But what do most of God's children do in such a situation?
>
> Often we stand by offering a lot of meaningless advice and some rather silly criticism.
>
> We even get impatient and try to help, and so get our hands in the Father's way, generally hindering the work ...
>
> Finally, in our desperation, we may even grab the toy out of the Father's hands entirely, saying rather bitterly that we hadn't really thought He could fix it anyway ... that we'd given Him a chance and He had failed us.[4]

The child-like faith of which Christ spoke is the kind which trusts the Father explicitly. The Father is given permission to do things His way with His timing because "We know that in all things God works for the good of those who love him ..."[5] The Bible does not teach that everything that happens to us is good, because it is not, yet God works in all things, even in the ashes of life, to bring good into our lives. Acceptance opens the way for His redemptive grace to work this miracle of miracles. The Apostle Paul knew this well when he wrote, "... I have learned to be content whatever the circumstances. I know what it is to be in need, and I know what it is to have plenty. I have learned the secret of being content in any and every situation, whether well fed or hungry, whether living in plenty or in want. I can do everything through him who gives me strength."[6] To keep any of us from missing the potency of Paul's statement, listen to the numerous opportunities he had to practice what he preached:

> "Five times I received from the Jews the forty lashes minus one. Three times I was beaten with rods, once I was stoned,

Acceptance

three times I was shipwrecked, I spent a night and a day in the open sea, I have been constantly on the move. I have been in danger from rivers, in danger from bandits, in danger from my own countrymen, in danger from Gentiles; in danger in the city, in danger in the country, in danger at sea, and in danger from false brothers. I have labored and toiled and have often gone without sleep; I have known hunger and thirst and have often gone without food; I have been cold and naked. Besides everything else, I face daily the pressure of my concern for all the churches."[7]

Does Paul's experience sound like a man who has had ample opportunity to test his faith or not? Paul found God's grace to be sufficient in his struggles and weaknesses and he both encourages us and inspires hope in us not only by what he wrote, but also by what he experienced. We can trust that kind of witness and can dare to believe that God will be adequate for us too.

Acceptance

Lord,
What an awesome burden choice becomes
   when life is encumbered with severe difficulties.
The existence of opposing options abound—
     Shall I turn and flee into the pseudo-shelter
       of denial?
     Shall I clinch my fist and fight angrily on?
     Or shall I open myself to face reality, no
       matter what?
When life thrusts a bitter cup into our hands
     It is one thing to pray, "Father, remove this
       cup from me,"
     And quite another to say, "Not my will, but
       thine be done."
The first is a longing flowing out of our humanity;
   the second, a commitment springing from our faith.
Give me the courage to commit myself fully to you,
   O God!

Lord,
How strange this peace which flows over me,
   even when everything external remains unchanged.
Can it be that I, rather than my circumstances, am
   being changed?
Could this transformation in me actually be the
   means through which my situation is altered?
It is for you alone to know, O Lord,
   and for me to trust.

Great are the mysteries of life in all parts of
   creation, and greater still the mystery of grace.
The butterfly, in straining to break free of the
   cocoon that now threatens the life it has
   protected, forces the vital fluids into its wings,
   thus strengthening its body for the flight ahead;

A flight made possible only by the struggle.
Surely the significance that can come from my
   struggle greatly exceeds that of the tiny butterfly.

Resignation to what I perceive to be my fate
   left me hopelessly defeated,
Whereas acceptance of the hard reality facing me
   has opened the door for peace to enter;
Peace born of a quiet confidence in you, O Lord,
   That I truly matter in your kingdom!
Above all, I have learned that
   No matter how deep the abyss,
     Your love is deeper still.

PART IV

The Hope

CHAPTER NINE

What Can I Expect from God?

We can expect God to be God at all times and in every situation. We cannot stereotype Him and say, "In this kind of circumstance He always does thus and so," because He does not always do "thus and so." He always loves us and He always desires the best for us, but He does not always rescue us the way we might expect. One scripture says of God:

> "For my thoughts are not your thoughts,
>   neither are your ways my ways,"
> declares the Lord.
>
> As the heavens are higher than the earth,
>   so are my ways higher than your ways
>   and my thoughts than your thoughts."[1]

Human logic runs along these lines: "If God truly loves me, He will prevent any harm from touching me; or, if pain comes, He will take it away when I ask Him to; or, when struggle comes with all its uncertainty, if He really loves me, He will smooth it out as quickly as I give Him permission to do so." Of course a closer look at our logic would reveal a desire for God to spoil us. What happens to a child whose parents give him everything he wants just when he wants it? That child never learns to cope with anything unpleasant and he does not develop inner discipline or strength of character. *God is not as interested in our having an easy life as in our having a great one.* This means that we can truly trust Him, for He is not a sadist enjoying our suffering but a Father who longs to give His children what is real and eternal.

The perspective established in the earlier chapters is that suffering exists because of the Fall. This means that we live in an abnormal world. We can by our own foolish actions increase our pain and the pain of others. However, not all suffering is the result of an individual's personal sin. Christ made that clear when his disciples asked concerning the blind man, " 'Rabbi, who sinned, this man or his parents, that he was born blind?' 'Neither this man nor his parents sinned,' said Jesus, 'but this happened so that the work of God might be displayed in his life'."[2]

Suffering comes to all of us some time or another, yet it need not be meaningless agony. In God's redemptive purpose suffering can become an opportunity for us to be transformed as we open ourselves to Him in that particular circumstance. As we noticed in the story of Job our struggle takes on the scope of a cosmic battle between God and Satan which is being fought in every man's life. So there is much more at stake here than we have ever dreamed.

C. S. Lewis pointed out that God whispers to us in our pleasures, He speaks to us in our consciousness and He shouts to us in our pain. I suppose we could say that pain guarantees that God will receive a second thought from us. We may resist the idea of coming to God out of dire circumstances, sort of as a last resort. Of course we can come to Him any time we become aware of His drawing us toward Himself. The problem is that most of us seem to enjoy too much the role of "playing God for ourselves" and resist giving up that foolish endeavor until we become desperate.

Awareness of our need for God and a willingness to give Him His proper place in our lives is all that is required of us. He certainly does not require our desperation, but many of us do.

It might help us to gain perspective if we note that, should God choose to eliminate the consequences of the Fall, He would in effect be lessening the significance of Adam and his freedom of choice. To destroy such freedom would lower the status of all mankind, an act which God refuses to perform. He chooses, instead, to work out His purposes within this environment. However, He does in His providence provide a tremendous amount of protection for each of us. Of all the things which could possibly go wrong in this fallen world, very little does, comparatively speaking.

As we struggle for some measure of understanding, it helps to remember that God Himself has entered into our suffering. He bore a cross in order to break the power of sin and to bring eternal life (which is a quality as well as a quantity of life) to all who believe. He understands suffering because He has been there and He, through the presence of His Holy Spirit, is here now going with us through our present struggles. We are not alone in an empty universe, a reality which has given untold comfort to those who have been open to His help in the midst of their agony. It also helps to remember that life as we know it now is not the whole story. The Christian has been given the eternal dimension as part of the total picture of existence.

Even with the general perspective that the Bible gives us regarding the problem of suffering, we must still acknowledge the presence of an enormous mystery as we deal with any particular experience of suffering. With the acknowledgement of mystery can also come the affirmation of meaning—*we matter and so does each experience through which we pass.*

We cannot put God in a box and use Him as we choose; we must instead be open to be taught by Him in each unique experience. We are given clues as to what we might expect from Him when we hurt. The Bible, which is the record of God's actions, gives us plenty of clues. The danger is that of focusing on one level of God's redemptive activity and trying to make that our sole expectation for His response in every situation. To do this is to set ourselves up for a tremendous disappointment, which may even cause us to doubt the validity of the Christian message. When we really notice the different ways that God has worked in the lives of his people, we are better able to build a solid base for our expectations.

As John Claypool points out, there are three distinct levels on which God may work in our lives. John's insight came from the biblical roots of his faith and from the loss of his ten-year-old daughter, Laura Lue, to leukemia. In his book, *Tracks Of A Fellow Struggler* he has written of his own pilgrimage through that dark place.

The most obvious level of God's intervention in our life is that of *rescue.* We want God to change the situation in some "miraculous" way. We will simply be the recipient of His gracious action. This is what we most often identify as the miraculous. Now, let there be no mistake about it, God does rescue us at times and in a way so obvious that we know "He did it," because we could not. John identifies this level as one of ecstasy, for so it is. To be in a bind and

What Can I Expect from God?

experience release through God's intervention is sheer exuberance. These experiences do come, thank God, at the most appropriate time.

The Bible is filled with illustrations of dramatic rescues. There was the time God brought the Hebrew people out of bondage in Egypt and they camped in the desert near the Red Sea. After the Israelites fled Egypt, Pharaoh had his heart hardened by the Lord (after he had hardened his own heart). The Lord gave him the strength to live out his original decision of defiance and, in so doing, revealed His mighty power to the world. Here is the story:

> As Pharaoh approached, the Israelites looked up, and there were the Egyptians, marching after them. They were terrified and cried out to the Lord. They said to Moses, "Was it because there were no graves in Egypt that you brought us to the desert to die? What have you done to us by bringing us out of Egypt? Didn't we say to you in Egypt, 'Leave us alone; let us serve the Egyptians'? It would have been better for us to serve the Egyptians than to die in the desert!"
>
> Moses answered the people, "Do not be afraid. Stand firm and you will see the deliverance the Lord will bring you today. The Egyptians you see today you will never see again. The Lord will fight for you; you need only to be still."[3]

The Lord did fight for them. The Red Sea parted and they escaped on dry ground. When the Egyptians pursued them the waters came together and drowned the entire army. No one but the Lord could pull off a rescue like that. And we can count on Him to rescue us when that is truly what we need for our good and for the fulfillment of His purpose.

Virginia, the woman mentioned in the first chapter, experienced a dramatic rescue. The entire family prayed for her healing and there was a sudden remission which even baffled her doctors. One doctor told her that his only explanation was that it must be a miracle. To be liberated from cancer, if only for four years, was an experience of ecstasy. I have known others and perhaps you have, also, who have experienced remission from the dreaded disease, never to have it return. But all of us must live each day as it comes. If the Lord tarries, we each will face death caused by something. So when God extends our days in such a manner that they can be enjoyed, we are blessed indeed.

We will, no doubt, pray and hope that God's action in our lives will be a quick rescue when hard times come upon us. There is absolutely nothing wrong with asking for such intervention. What does create a problem, though, is to fail to recognize God's work in our situation when it is not an overt act of deliverance. To identify the presence or absence of God as being synonymous with either a quick rescue or unchanged circumstances is to misunderstand altogether.

Again, the Israelites illustrate this quite well. When they followed Moses out of Egypt and across the Red Sea they expected an easy trip to the land which flowed with milk and honey. When they arrived in the desert the sand was hot, the children were crying, and water was scarce. They naturally assumed that the presence of problems meant the absence of God. That seems to be a common human assumption. Yet God was with them in the tough part of their journey in a way that ultimately, could be the most help. Those people had been slaves all their lives. They did not know how to live as free men. God was giving them some desert training to toughen them so they could possess the land that He was going to give them. Although it felt like neglect on God's part, it was really His love

What Can I Expect from God?

working to give them their best chance to really be somebody—a people of faith who could endure the discipline and become as no other nation, the great servants of mankind.

Unfortunately, they never grasped that truth and refused to accept anything other than dramatic rescue as God's only level of intervention. Their faith never grew and when the test came at the Jordan, after the twelve spies gave their report about the "promised land," they failed miserably. God had given them one miracle after another. They had no reason not to trust Him explicitly. He had given them plenty of experiences for building a solid foundation of faith. The story follows:

> The Lord said to Moses, "Send some men to explore the land of Canaan, which I am giving to the Israelites . . ."[4]
>
> They came back to Moses and Aaron and the whole Israelite community at Kadesh in the Desert of Paran. There they reported to them and to the whole assembly and showed them the fruit of the land. They gave Moses this account: "We went into the land to which you sent us, and it does flow with milk and honey! Here is its fruit. But the people who live there are powerful, and the cities are fortified and very large. We even saw descendants of Anak there . . .
>
> Then Caleb silenced the people before Moses and said, "We should go up and take possession of the land, for we can certainly do it."
>
> But the men who had gone up with him said, "We can't attack those people; they are stronger than we are." And they spread among the Israelites a bad report . . . "We seemed like grasshoppers in our own eyes, and we looked the same to them."
>
> That night all the people of the community raised their voices and wept aloud. All the Israelites grumbled against

Moses and Aaron, and the whole assembly said to them, "If only we had died in Egypt! Or in the desert! Why is the Lord bringing us to this land only to let us fall by the sword ... We should choose a leader and go back to Egypt."[5]

Fear can do terrible things to us. When the spies reported, "We seemed like grasshoppers in our own eyes," we know how great was their fear. *Fear causes us to underestimate our own resources and to doubt the care and power of God.* It was not the enemy in the land that was their problem; it was the enemy within.

The greatest battles that we will ever fight are those within ourselves. When the pressure mounts and we are tempted to take matters into our own hands and to cry out against God or to flee into despair, then we know how much we desperately need to open ourselves to Him for the strength which He alone can give.

The Hebrews expected God to give them the land without any struggle on their part. But He was calling them to participate with Him in conquering the land. In that participation they could become more than if God had done everything for them. We are so drawn to the "easy" life that we, too, resist the prospect of struggle and are tempted to look for magic in our religion rather than God's kind of miracles. If it is magic we expect from God, we are going to be disillusioned. If it is meaning and purpose, strength and character, love and greatness we expect from Him in the midst of our difficulties, then we will not be disappointed ultimately. He always comes to help us, but as One who sees the end from the beginning—One who has eternity incorporated into His perspective. He may rescue us, and if He does, we can be certain that is what we needed and we can praise Him for it. But rescue is *His* option, not ours!

What Can I Expect from God?

The second and most common level of God's intervention is that of *collaboration*. That is, He includes us as participants with Him in the miraculous process of meeting our needs, but in such a way as to give us maximum opportunities for developing great strength of character. At this level He does not do it for us but with us. He simply works with us so that we can help change the circumstances for ourselves, for in no other way can we ever come to any significant degree of maturity.

God's love for us is too great to allow us to be mere spectators. Rather, He calls us to full participation in life with Him. This is the adventure for which every human heart hungers. God has designed a place for us in His eternal purpose but not a place which eliminates our freedom or causes us to operate in a closed system. Our choices, responses and actions have major consequences on both the history of man and the purpose of God. Each life is of infinite value and God takes us all very seriously.

Virginia's story shows that she was a full participant in the miracles God brought into her life. She and Ted sought the best medical help they could find. She dealt honestly with her trauma and her feelings and fought for life with all the resources available. Virginia did not give up in self pity. She did what she could, she allowed others to help, and she trusted God. She submitted herself to strenuous examinations periodically by physicians who were making a special study of her case in the hope that what they learned could be used to help others. The impact of her life blessed everyone who knew her. In a very real sense Virginia became a miracle of love, of faith and of life.

The experience of David and Goliath in the Old Testament illustrates collaboration beautifully. The army of the Philistines occupied one hill and the Israelites another. Each day for forty days the Philistine champion, Goliath, challenged the Hebrews to send out their best warrior to do combat with him. The Bible tells us that this Philistine was over nine feet tall and wore a coat of armor weighing 150 pounds and that he carried a spear with an iron point weighing eighteen pounds. Goliath's very appearance struck fear into the hearts of the men of Israel and none were willing to accept his challenge, a fact not hard to understand.

I am certain that there were those among the Israelites who prayed for God to do something about this vulgar enemy who mocked both the armies of Saul and the God of Israel. If God would intervene by striking this pagan with lightning or some such phenomenon, then all Israel would know that the Lord fought for them. God could have done so, just as He led the children of Israel out of Egypt and across the Red Sea by His mighty acts. Yet here God has something else in mind—the miracle of a finite man trusting God sufficiently to risk doing something about this situation himself. Since God has the power to do as He pleases, it is a greater miracle to work in a man who has the choice of saying, "No, I won't risk it" and enabling that man to accomplish that which he is willing to attempt by sheer faith.

Prayer for deliverance should never be underestimated. Yet had everyone simply prayed for rescue without anyone acting on faith to find out if God would answer their prayer, then Goliath would not have been defeated. God acted decisively in and through a young man who himself was willing to bet his life on God. Someone had to cross that valley, face that giant and find out, if, in reality God would help defeat the enemy. David was that man! He took the external weapons that fit him best, along with the inner knowledge that God had delivered him from the

What Can I Expect from God?

paws of the lion and the bear as he cared for his father's sheep. He believed that God had taken care of him in the past and would do so now, especially since Goliath had cursed the God of Israel. In his hands he carried a sling, but in his heart he had a faith which said, "The battle is the Lord's and I give Him permission this day to use me as He chooses."

From the world's point of view the odds were definitely in Goliath's favor, but from faith's point of view Goliath never had a chance. Still, someone had to act on that faith to find out for sure.

Goliath was furious when he saw David because he knew there would be no real glory for him in killing a boy. The drama unfolds:

> ... the Philistine, with his shield bearer in front of him kept coming closer to David. He looked David over and saw that he was only a boy, ruddy and handsome, and he despised him. He said to David, "Am I a dog, that you come at me with sticks?" And the Philistine cursed David by his gods. "Come here," he said, "and I'll give your flesh to the birds of the air and the beasts of the field!"
>
> David said to the Philistine, "You come against me with sword and spear and javelin, but I come against you in the name of the Lord Almighty, the God of the Armies of Israel, whom you have defied. This day the Lord will hand you over to me, and I'll strike you down and cut off your head. Today I will give the carcasses of the Philistine army to the birds of the air and the beasts of the earth, and the whole world will know that there is a God in Israel. All those gathered here will know that it is not by sword or spear that the Lord saves; for the battle is the Lord's, and he will give all of you into our hands."
>
> As the Philistine moved closer to attack him, David ran quickly toward the battle line to meet him. Reaching into his

bag and taking out a stone, he slung it and struck the Philistine on the forehead. The stone sank into his forehead, and he fell facedown on the ground.

So David triumphed over the Philistine with a sling and a stone; without a sword in his hand he struck down the Philistine and killed him.

David ran and stood over him. He took hold of the Philistine's sword and drew it from the scabbard. After he killed him, he cut off his head with the sword.

When the Philistines saw that their hero was dead, they turned and ran."[6]

Let me point out that David had such faith that the Lord would help him that he aggressively carried the fight to Goliath. The scripture says "David ran quickly toward the battle line . . ." This was an act of total abandonment of one's life and destiny to God. With David, it was "all or none"! David actively collaborated with God in this miracle and two things happened simultaneously: first, all knew that truly God had intervened in this battle; secondly, David, the boy, became a man with an incredible future because He had dared to believe God.

It should be obvious why God moves more often on the level of collaboration. Not only does He reveal Himself but He also does something great in the person who risks with Him. That is more in line with God's nature and His purpose. We share with Him in such a way that His kind of character is formed in us in the process. This means that we are not automats, but human beings who are in a real sense partial architects of our own life and destiny. We have a lot to say about what becomes of us. We can thank God for that incredible gift and for the hope which comes in recognizing that *it is God who is the final architect.*

What Can I Expect from God?

In the New Testament, when Jesus entered his home town of Nazareth and began to teach, he was not accepted by the people: "... Jesus said to them, 'Only in his home town and in his own house is a prophet without honor.' And he did not do many miracles there because of their lack of faith."[7] Because they knew his mother and his brothers and had known him as the carpenter's son, they were offended that he would attempt to teach them. Familiarity with only part of the reality surrounding his life led to contempt. They knew him well on the appearance level, but not well enough on the personal level to believe. Without openness on their part (collaboration) He did few miracles there. We can open or close the door on God's actions in our life by either a willing heart or a skeptical spirit.

A practical summary of this level of God's intervention would be to say, "Do all that you know to do, leave no stones unturned and trust God to do for you, in you and through you what only He can do."

John Claypool identifies the third level of God's intervention in our lives as *endurance*. Here is his witness:

> Fortunately, there is one other form that the promise of God's strength takes: "They shall walk and not faint." Now I am sure that to those looking for the spectacular this may sound insignificant indeed. Who wants to be slowed to a walk, to creep along inch by inch, just barely above the threshold of consciousness and not fainting? That may not sound like much of a religious experience, but believe me, in the kind of darkness where I have been, it is the only form of the promise that fits the situation...
>
> The hardest thing of all for me in the last two weeks has been my helplessness in the face of Laura Lue's suffering. If

only there had been something I could have done to change things tangibly, it would have been easier—but there was not . . . . . . I was given the strength "to walk and not faint."

The least of gifts, you say? Maybe so, from one standpoint, yet in another way, it was the most appropriate of all gifts, the one thing most needful in that situation. And because I was willing to settle for it—so little yet so much, I can say honestly: my religion did make a difference when the bottom dropped out. It kept me from giving up! . . .

Well, that is how it was, and here I am this morning—sad, broken-hearted, still bearing in my spirit the wounds of the darkness. I confess to you honestly that I have no wings with which to fly or even any legs on which to run—but listen, by the grace of God, *I am still on my feet!* I have not fainted yet. I have not exploded in the anger of presumption, nor have I keeled over into the paralysis of despair. All I am doing is walking and not fainting, hanging in there, enduring with patience what I cannot change but have to bear.[8]

In facing the cross Christ Himself prayed, "Father, if you are willing, take this cup from me; yet not my will, but yours be done."[9] Christ was facing something He could not change and remain true to the redemptive purpose of the Father. He simply had to *endure* that cross, but in His endurance the Father has exalted Him above every name and has made forgiveness and new life available to everyone who will accept Him by faith.

As the Psalmist wrote:

God is our refuge and strength,
    an ever present help in trouble.
Therefore we will not fear, though the earth give way
    and the mountains fall into the heart of the sea,
though its waters roar and foam
    and the mountains quake with their surging.

What Can I Expect from God?

The Lord Almighty is with us;
   the God of Jacob is our fortress.[10]

God is with us, and He does help us. But the way He helps us in a given situation is for us to discover as we move with Him through the shadows into the light of His love and grace.

At some point each of us, too, will face a situation from which there is no rescue and nothing we can do on our own or with God's help will change it. If Christ tarries, death will be one of those stark realities. We may be rescued from that grim experience many times but the day will inevitably come when we will no longer need God's protective grace or His healing grace; we will need His dying grace! Death is not the only experience which we may face that we cannot change and for which we need an extra portion of God's grace. For some it may be divorce; for others it may be the loss of a job or position; an accident which robs us of the use of our limbs; an illness which incapacitates us some way; a close relationship which carries deep pain; a life-long dream which must be abandoned. Sometimes endurance, to be able "to walk and not faint," is the gift we most need for the present circumstances.

Virginia's experience was one of acceptance and endurance in the end. In her first round with cancer she experienced a dramatic rescue in the form of a four-year remission, as an answer to their prayers. For the second occurrance of cancer there was found no reprieve, even though her family and her doctors did all they could. Virginia struggled with the grim prospect of death, moving through the process described earlier. She realized that with her situation growing more acute each week, if anything changed it would be her, not her circumstances. As she accepted the reality of what lay ahead she began to turn loose of the things and the people that she knew she could not hold on to, coming finally to the place that she could say, "Why not me?" Even as the apostle Paul had learned to accept life where he was having to live it, so had Virginia.

Virginia's husband came to faith in Christ out of what he saw in the living and dying witness of the wife he loved so deeply. In his livingroom sometime later, with tears flowing down his cheeks, he shared with me, "You know, that woman loved me so much that, had she known that this is what it would take to bring me into God's kingdom, she would have gladly chosen to endure it." Virginia's suffering had eternal significance and meaning far beyond what we, with our limited perspective, can ever envision. Thank God for the Virginias who have endured and in so doing have inspired hope in us all.

What Can I Expect from God?

And we know that in all things God works for
 the good of those who love him . . .

What, then, shall we say in response to this?
 If God is for us, who can be against us?
He who did not spare his own Son, but gave
 him up for us all—how will he not also,
 along with him, graciously give us all things? . . .

Who shall separate us from the love of Christ?
 Shall trouble or hardship or persecution or
 famine or nakedness or danger or sword? . . .

No, in all these things we are more than conquerors
 through him who loves us.
For I am convinced that neither death nor life, neither
 angels nor demons, neither the present nor the
 future, nor any powers, neither height nor depth,
 nor anything else in all creation,
Will be able to separate us from the love of God
 that is in Christ Jesus our Lord.
      From Romans 8:28, 31-32, 35, 37-39

PART V

Personal Reflection/ Group Interaction

The purpose of this section is twofold: first, to help those who have read this book to make personal application of the biblical truths herein and secondly, to furnish dialogue questions for those who would use this book as the basis for a supportive sharing group. Each question/answer section can be used for a session. I would encourage those in such groups to make their sharing personal rather than theoretical and impersonal—express your own feelings, fears, hopes and spiritual direction along with the things you or someone close to you has found most helpful. It is important to answer each question for yourself, but each should only share what they feel comfortable with in that particular session.

The Christian journey was intended to be made in the company of other committed men and women where mutual encouragement, support and accountability exist. Small groups within the community of faith seem to be one of the most potent vehicles for stimulating discovery and spiritual growth. Christ, Himself, modeled for us the potential effectiveness of small groups when He chose to work most intimately with twelve disciples.

SESSION ONE

No one can live long without encountering suffering—our own or that of someone close to us, which also causes anguish for us.

1. What would you identify as your greatest struggle?
2. Did you try to handle that situation in any nonproductive ways?
3. How did your models (parents and others close to you) handle their difficult situations?
4. How well did their method work for them from your perspective now?
5. What was the turning point for you, if there has been one?
6. List the people who were most helpful to you and the things they did.
7. Did you make any vows or develop any strong feelings about what you would or would not do in a similar situation or what you would do to avoid the possibility of getting in that situation again?
8. Have you kept your vows? How well have they served you? Have they created any new problems? Do you now feel you need to change any of those vows?

9. Is there anything about yourself or your situation that you would like to change?
10. What seems the best direction to take for change to occur?
11. What would you identify as a current struggle for you?
12. Are you open for outside help (such as God, friends, a counselor)?
13. What do you need most from this group?
14. What would you most like to give to this group?

SESSION TWO

What I bring to both the opportunities and struggles of life is *myself.* Try as I may, I cannot escape me. If I do not like me, the only thing I can do is open myself to God in a serious way for Him to enable me to either change and/or come to a healthy self-acceptance.

1. On a scale from 0 to 10 with the larger number representing the more positive score, what score would you give yourself in the area of self-esteem? What do you perceive as some of the things which have helped your self-esteem? What are some things which have hindered?
2. Describe the way you think others perceive you.
3. How would you describe yourself? What are the best things you can say about yourself? What would you like to change?
4. Is there any particular trait or characteristic of yours which contributes to conflict with others? How did this pattern develop? Did either of your parents respond in this manner?
5. Are you a complainer? Why or why not?
6. Do you see yourself as a victim of circumstances

beyond your control most of the time; some of the time; none of the time?

7. Do you find it all too easy to blame others for your problems? When did this pattern begin, or what have you done to keep from falling into this trap?
8. When you fail at something important is it easier to say: "It's not my fault—he/she/they are to blame"; "I am a failure"; or "I have failed in this particular endeavor"?
9. When you have the wind knocked out of your sail personally, how quick do you usually bounce back? Have you ever had a devastating experience that took a long time for recovery? Are you a stronger person for having survived such an ordeal? In what way are you stronger?
10. What discoveries have you made about yourself from your struggle?
11. What discoveries have you made about God from these struggles?

SESSION THREE

Faith's first step toward release is honesty with ourselves and with God about what is going on inside of us. Refusal to deal realistically with our feelings can leave a root of bitterness which may become an inner wedge between ourselves and God. Opening up allows God's healing grace to enter. In dealing with our emotions we need also to keep in mind the fact that there are no *good* or *bad* emotions in a moral sense, only authentic feelings which must be dealt with in a healthy way. Once we choose to express those feelings we may do so in a positive or negative, constructive or destructive manner. The way we choose to express our emotions does take on moral connotations because we can hurt or help ourselves and others by the way we express the feelings stirring within.

1. What do you do with your "unacceptable" feelings? Deny them? Repress them and stew inside? Blow up and pour your displeasure on others? Or seek a positive release?
2. What have you found that works best for you as a positive release for your strong "negative" emotions?
3. Have you ever truly accepted your own humanity with potential for doing both good or evil? Can you accept

yourself as a fallible human being, or are you a perfectionist with little tolerance for your own mistakes or for the mistakes of others? What would it take for you to genuinely accept yourself?

4. Who would you identify as the one person who knows you better than anyone else? Why have you revealed yourself so thoroughly to that particular person? Has it been easy or hard for you to let that person really know you? Why?

5. When you pray do you find it easy or hard to pour out your true feelings to God? The Psalmist prayed, "Why, O Lord, do you stand far off? Why do you hide yourself in times of trouble?" Those were his true feelings at that particular moment. God had not hidden Himself, but the anguish which the Psalmist felt caused him to feel that God was absent from the situation. Honest dialogue with God offers the greatest hope for God's help to be most effective. Remember, prayer is a two way dialogue—waiting and listening to the Lord is of utmost importance.

6. Would you feel comfortable being that open with God about what you are feeling? Why? Try it for 30 days and report back to the group.

SESSION FOUR

To be confronted with unexpected circumstances which bring more pain—physical and/or emotional—than we are prepared to take in leaves us in utter shock. Such shock causes us to be disoriented. While in such a state our minds are not capable of fully grasping the reality thrust upon us. Time, patience and understanding helps us move more easily out of our disorientation and into constructive action.

1. Have you ever experienced shock? What was it like for you?
2. How long were you in that state?
3. What and/or who helped you to move out of your shock and into some constructive action?
4. What would you recommend others do when they are trying to be helpful to the person who is in a state of shock?

SESSION FIVE

The more intense a person's struggle, the more one is driven to seek the *why* of it. The search for the *why* may lead to some important discoveries, but the real issue in suffering is not *why* but what will be our response.

1. Have you ever been tempted to respond to some crisis with presumption—getting so frustrated with God that you take things into your own hands and explode in some fit of rage? Did you? What calmed you down?
2. Have you ever been tempted to respond to a difficult situation by giving up altogether and dissolving in despair? Did you? What caused you to try again?
3. Have you ever felt like crying out, "Why me? What have I done?" How did you handle those feelings?
4. Have you ever traveled the road of *unquestioning resignation* in dealing with your problems? How did it work?
5. Have you ever traveled the road of *pursuing total intellectual understanding* in dealing with your problems? Did you ever totally understand?
6. Have you ever tried to face a major crisis in your life by taking the road of *gratitude?* How did it work?

7. Have you ever experienced an overwhelming sense of fear: fear of pain; fear that this situation will alter your life so drastically that nothing will ever be the same again; fear that you may not be able to cope with the situation or accept it; fear of failure; fear of losing control and of becoming dependent; fear of losing self respect and/or the respect of others, or fear of losing your place or your power or your worth?
8. What helped you to overcome your fear?
9. What kind of things make you most angry? What do you do with your anger?
10. Would you rather be bitter, or tender and sensitive? What choices can you make which will help you avoid the pitfall of bitterness and enable you to be a sensitive, loving person?

SESSION SIX

For those of us who believe that God is, it is quite natural that we try every means available to get Him to help make everything alright again when we are in a difficult place. Others who never thought seriously about God one way or another usually do so when the going gets tough enough. All men are finite and as such are driven to seek the Infinite when there is a serious threat to one's survival— physically, emotionally, relationally, economically, or in any other area that is of great importance. Being driven to seek God out of dire circumstances is not to be frowned upon. It is a healthy response to the reality of man's finiteness. It makes no sense to resist the greatest source of help man has, especially when the circumstances of his life have crushed every illusion that he is self-sufficient.

1. Have you ever made a serious beginning with God? Have you ever committed as much of yourself as you could to as much of Jesus Christ as you understood? Why or Why Not?
2. What led to your decision to commit your life to Christ?
3. Who influenced you the most to make such commitment?

4. What did it take to make you aware of your own finiteness? What crushed your illusion of self-sufficiency, if it indeed has been crushed?
5. Do you understand that although everything which happens to you is not good God is capable of bringing good out of all things for you? (Romans 8:28) Such realization will help us trust Him and enable us to open our difficult situations to Him more quickly.
6. Have you ever made promises to God which you hoped would cause Him to intervene on your behalf in some situation?
7. Are you willing to trust God to work in your situation even when He is not doing things your way? Would you ask Him to help you trust Him completely with your life?

SESSION SEVEN

In the midst of struggle, when nothing seems to be working to bring relief, most will experience a degree of depression. It comes when the feeling exists that there is nothing left to do that will make any difference. The more intense and serious the "unsolvable" problem is, the greater the possibility for despondency.

1. Have you ever attempted to identify your own mood swing patterns? What usually causes you to feel flat or despondent?
2. What have you found helpful for elevating your mood?
3. Have you learned the difference between false guilt and true guilt? What do you do when you discover that you are experiencing false guilt? What do you do when you discover that you are experiencing true guilt?
4. If we ask God to forgive us and the guilt lingers, then we need to ask Him to help us forgive ourselves because He has already done so. Why do you suppose it is so hard for us to forgive ourselves?
5. How can our memory help us better cope with our current despair?
6. Can you identify at least one of God's promises which could give you encouragement and support during your struggle?

SESSION EIGHT

Acceptance of life's hard places is one of God's most profound gifts to us humans. With a disposition prone to rebellion and an insatiable attraction to the "easy" life, our "normal" reaction to threat is to kick and scream. We want immediate relief or, better yet, not even the possibility of pain. Yet acceptance of the hard reality facing us opens the door for peace to enter. Acceptance comes easier to the fighter because he first explores all the possibilities for change he can find; resignation comes more readily to those who have a tendency to give up without much fight.

1. Can you see that what we and those who love us may learn in our struggles may bring us closer to understanding the very essence of our existence? If life were to always be easy, how sensitive would we be; how appreciative; how supportive of others?
2. Do you see value in accepting what we cannot change and in turning loose of what we cannot keep? It does not come easy, does it?
3. What distinction would you make between *resignation* and *acceptance* in this context?

4. What situation have you encountered that simply could not be changed? How did you cope with it or how are you coping with it? (Remember Paul's thorn in the flesh—II Corinthians 12:7-10)
5. How can a demanding spirit prevent the grace of God from enabling us to reach that emotional and spiritual solace called acceptance?
6. Have you learned the secret of contentment—the kind Paul speaks of in Philippians 4:11-13?
7. Can you pray, "Lord, let your will be done even if it is totally contrary to my present desires?" Ask Him to help you to be able to sincerely pray that prayer, and give Him time to do it.
8. Can you recall an experience of *acceptance* in which you felt tremendous relief? What steps did you take which ultimately led to this?

SESSION NINE

God is not as concerned with our having an easy life as with our having a great one. This means that we can truly trust Him, for He is not a sadist enjoying our struggles but a Father who longs to give His children what is real and eternal. As we learned from the story of Job, our struggles take on the scope of a cosmic battle which is being fought in every person's life.

1. Have you ever experienced a "miracle"—one of rescue; one of collaboration; one of endurance? What impact have these made on your life?
2. Have you ever felt that God failed to come through for you when you needed Him most? Was the problem with God or with your expectations? Were you expecting God to only intervene in some form of dramatic rescue? Can you understand the situation better now?
3. Identify reasons you believe you have for personally trusting God even when you can neither understand why certain things are happening nor can you see God at work in them.
4. Have you ever seriously accepted the fact that God

knows you by name and has a significant purpose for your life?

5. What do you consider to be your greatest resources for handling your difficult situations?
6. Have you ever done something and afterwards realized that you could not have done that without a tremendous amount of help from God Himself?
7. Does it challenge or frighten you to realize that you are in a very real sense partial architect of your own life and destiny? Our choices, our actions, our attitudes and our commitments contribute enormously to who and what we become. We can be grateful, though, that God is the final architect.
8. Has familiarity with the words of the gospel had a dulling effect on you as to the incredible truth of those words? (For example, to talk about love without truly loving robs the word of its potency.)
9. What have you found most helpful for keeping the truth of the gospel alive in your own life?
10. Would you dare to ask the Living Christ to give you a love for Him and for His redemptive purpose that runs deeper than the love of your own life? That is the greatest of all gifts and the one which equips us best for living as God's people in this world.

Chapter 1 . . . "An Agony Too Deep for Words"

1. C. S. Lewis, A GRIEF OBSERVED, England: Faber and Faber Limited, 1961, p. 25.
2. Philippians 3:7-8, summary
3. Philippians 3:10a, paraphrased.
4. John 14:27. All Scripture is from the NEW INTERNATIONAL VERSION. Grand Rapids, Michigan: Zondervan Publishing House, 1978.
5. Hebrews 9:27
6. John 11:25
7. I Corinthians 15:26
8. I Corinthians 15:54b-57
9. C. S. Lewis, pp. 4-5
10. Ibid., p. 38.

Chapter 2 . . . "What Am I Bringing to the Struggle"

1. Edith Schaeffer, AFFLICTIONS, Old Tappan, New Jersey: Fleming H. Revell Company, 1978, p. 75.
2. Job 1:20-22
3. Job 2:4-6
4. Job 2:9-10
5. Job 4:8
6. Job 8:3-6
7. Job 11:13-15
8. Job 7:16b and Job 3:26
9. Job 21:23a-26a
10. Job 7:20b
11. Job 6:15a
12. Job 7:4
13. Job 9:25
14. Job 12:4a, 5a
15. Job 16:2-3a, 4a, 13:5
16. Job 14:1
17. Job 19:7
18. Job 19:4
19. Job
20. Job 23:3a, 8-9
21. Job 13:15
22. Job 42:3b; 5
23. Francis Bacon, NOVUM ORGANUM SCIENTIARUM (1620).

Chapter 3 . . . "Let the Heart Speak"

1. Revelation 21:4
2. C. S. Lewis, A GRIEF OBSERVED, p. 5 and p. 34.
3. Ibid., p. 35.

Chapter 4 . . . "There Must Be Some Mistake"

1. Job 2:12-13

Chapter 5 . . . "Why Me?"

1. Psalm 130:1-2
2. Psalm 10:1
3. Psalm 13:1-2
4. Psalm 6:1-3, 6-7
5. John Claypool, TRACKS OF A FELLOW STRUGGLER, Waco, Texas: Word Books, 1974, pp. 53-54.
6. Psalm 13:6
7. John Claypool, p. 61.

Chapter 6 . . . "Promises"

1. Philippians 4:6-7
2. Romans 8:28
3. Joni Eareckson's complete story is told in her book JONI, Grand Rapids, Michigan: Zondervan Publishing House, 1976.
4. Philip Yancey, WHERE IS GOD WHEN IT HURTS, Grand Rapids, Michigan: Zondervan Publishing House, 1977, pp. 119-120.

Chapter 7 . . . "What's the Use?"

1. Kenneth Hildebrand, ACHIEVING REAL HAPPINESS, New York: Harper and Brothers, 1955, p. 139.
2. Tim LaHaye, HOW TO WIN OVER DEPRESSION, Grand Rapids, Michigan: Zondervan Publishing House, 1974, p. 35.
3. Psalm 32:1-5, 11a
4. I Corinthians 10:13a
5. C. S. Lewis, A GRIEF OBSERVED, pp. 3-4, p. 9.
6. Psalm 5:1-2
7. Psalm 42:5-7
8. I Corinthians 10:13b

Notes

Chapter 8 ... "Acceptance"

1. Catherine Marshall, BEYOND OURSELVES, New York: McGraw Hill, 1961, pp. 103.
2. Ibid., 104.
3. Luke 18:16b-17
4. Catherine Marshall, p. 98-99.
5. Romans 8:28a
6. Philippians 4:11b-13
7. II Corinthians 11:24-28

Chapter 9 ... "What Can I Expect from God?"

1. Isaiah 55:8-9
2. John 9:2-3a
3. Exodus 14:10-14
4. Numbers 13:1-2a
5. Numbers 13:26-14:4
6. I Samuel 17:41-51
7. Matthew 13:57b-58
8. John Claypool, TRACKS OF A FELLOW STRUGGLER, pp. 52, 54, 57.
9. Luke 22:42
10. Psalm 46:1-3, 7